T0017271

MEDITATIONS

Also available in the same series:

Beyond Good and Evil: The Philosophy Classic by Friedrich Nietzsche (ISBN: 978-0-857-08848-2)

On the Origin of Species: The Science Classic by Charles Darwin (ISBN: 978-0-857-08847-5)

Tao Te Ching: The Ancient Classic by Lao Tzu (ISBN: 978-0-857-08311-1)

The Art of War: The Ancient Classic by Sun Tzu (ISBN: 978-0-857-08009-7)

The Game of Life and How to Play It: The Self-Help Classic by Florence Scovel Shinn (ISBN: 978-0-857-08840-6)

The Interpretation of Dreams: The Psychology Classic by Sigmund Freud (ISBN: 978-0-857-08844-4)

The Prince: The Original Classic by Niccolo Machiavelli (ISBN: 978-0-857-08078-3)

The Prophet: The Spirituality Classic by Kahlil Gibran (ISBN: 978-0-857-08855-0)

The Republic: The Influential Classic by Plato (ISBN: 978-0-857-08313-5)

The Science of Getting Rich: The Original Classic by Wallace Wattles (ISBN: 978-0-857-08008-0)

The Wealth of Nations: The Economics Classic by Adam Smith (ISBN: 978-0-857-08077-6)

Think and Grow Rich: The Original Classic by Napoleon Hill (ISBN: 978-1-906-46559-9)

MEDITATIONS
The Philosophy Classic

MARCUS AURELIUS

With an Introduction by
DONALD ROBERTSON

CAPSTONE
A Wiley Brand

Registered office
John Wiley & Sons Ltd, The Atrium, Southern Gate, Chichester, West Sussex, PO19 8SQ, United Kingdom

For details of our global editorial offices, for customer services and for information about how to apply for permission to reuse the copyright material in this book please see our website at www.wiley.com.

A catalogue record for this book is available from the Library of Congress.

A catalogue record for this book is available from the British Library.

ISBN 978–0–857–08846–8 (hardback) ISBN 978–0–857–08849–9 (ePDF)
ISBN 978–0–857–08841–3 (ePub)

C9780857088468_140623

Cover design: Wiley

Set in 11/15pt ITC New Baskerville by Aptara, New Delhi, India
Printed in Great Britain by CPI Group (UK) Ltd, Croydon CR0 4YY

CONTENTS

AN INTRODUCTION

BY DONALD ROBERTSON

> "If thou would'st master care and pain,
> Unfold this book and read and read again
> Its blessed leaves, whereby thou soon shalt see
> The past, the present, and the days to be
> With opened eyes; and all delight, all grief,
> Shall be like smoke, as empty and as brief."

This epigram is found at the end of a Vatican manuscript of *The Meditations* of Marcus Aurelius. It captures the central appeal of the book, which is that it offers a way to "master care and pain" by providing philosophical insights that promise to elevate our minds above worldly concerns – both the things we crave and those we fear.

The Stoic wisdom *The Meditations* contains offers us a whole philosophy of life, capable of providing a much-needed sense of purpose and direction in the modern world – just as it did nearly two thousand years ago for people living in the Roman Empire.

THE PHILOSOPHER KING

Marcus Aurelius was the last famous Stoic philosopher of antiquity. He also happens to have been emperor of Rome during the height of its power. As a consequence, we know considerably more about him than about any other Stoic philosopher. We have accounts of Marcus' life and reign from Cassius Dio, Herodian, and the *Historia Augusta* – a history of the Roman emperors – as well as fragments of evidence from other historical sources.

The Meditations itself opens with a series of remarks about his family members and teachers, and the nature of the text – a series of private notes on his endeavours to apply Stoic philosophy in his own life – gives us some glimpses of Marcus' personal concerns. In addition, we have a cache of letters between Marcus and his Latin rhetoric tutor, and close family friend, Marcus Cornelius Fronto, which provide a window on his character and personal life.

Marcus wasn't the sort of decadent autocrat that many people today associate with the immensely privileged position of Roman emperor. For example, Herodian writes of him:

> *He was concerned with all aspects of excellence, and in his love of ancient literature he was second to no man, Roman or Greek; this is evident from all his sayings and writings which have come down to us. To his subjects he revealed himself as a mild and moderate emperor; he gave audience to those who asked for it and forbade his bodyguard to drive off those who happened to meet him. Alone of the emperors, he gave proof of his learning not by mere words or knowledge of philosophical doctrines but by his blameless character and temperate way of life. His reign thus produced a very large number of intelligent men, for subjects like to imitate the example set by their ruler.*

We're told that he constantly had the saying of Plato on his lips, "that those states prospered where the philosophers were kings or the kings philosophers" (*Historia Augusta*). Indeed, by all accounts he was widely perceived as embodying the principles of the Stoic philosophy that he followed, and which he describes throughout *The Meditations*.

Curiously, Marcus never mentions the word 'Stoic' anywhere in the text, although there's no question that he considered himself a follower of that school's teachings. The Roman historian, Cassius Dio, says that although Marcus had tutors in Platonic and Aristotelian philosophy, "he was most inclined to the doctrines of the Stoic school". The two philosophers he cites most often in the book are Epictetus – perhaps unsurprisingly, as he was the most important Stoic teacher of the Roman world – and Heraclitus, a famous pre-Socratic philosopher who appears to have influenced the Stoics. Marcus also mentions two other "noble philosophers" favoured by the Stoics, Socrates and Pythagoras (6.47). Curiously, Marcus nowhere mentions Zeno, the founder of the Stoic school, but he does mention Chrysippus, the third head of the Stoic school, alongside Socrates and Epictetus: "How many a Chrysippus, how many a Socrates, how many an Epictetus has time already swallowed up!", he writes (7.19).

The *Historia Augusta* describes Marcus as being "wholly given over to the Stoic philosophy, which he had not only learned from all the best masters, but also acquired for himself from every source". Indeed, Marcus was well-known for having dedicated his life to training in Stoic philosophy, a path which he started upon from the unusually young age of twelve. This commitment is summed up in the *Historia Augusta*:

> For the emperor was so illustrious in philosophy that when he was about to set out for the Marcomannic war, and everyone was fearful that some ill-luck might befall him, he was asked, not in flattery but in all seriousness, to publish his "Precepts of Philosophy"; and he did not fear to do so, but for three days discussed the books of his "Exhortations" one after the other.

It's not clear whether or not these "Precepts of Philosophy" or "Exhortations", if real, correspond with *The Meditations*, his only surviving philosophical text. As we'll see, the content of *The Meditations* consists mainly of notes to himself on philosophical themes rather than formal precepts or exhortations.

It seems unlikely that *The Meditations* was ever intended for publication. Marcus frequently alludes to events that would be obscure or meaningless to most people reading it, even people of his time – such as the contents of a letter received by his mother, or a dispute his adoptive father had with a customs officer. He also criticizes his own character quite harshly and complains about the values of those surrounding him at court. These are remarks he presumably would have intended to keep to himself. If the *Historia Augusta* is correct, therefore, it may be that Marcus published some other philosophical writings that are now lost.

In any case, it seems clear that to subsequent generations of Romans, and perhaps during his own lifetime, Marcus had earned the reputation of a ruler who aspired to, and arguably succeeded in nearing, the ancient Platonic ideal of the philosopher-king.

TO HIMSELF

The title *Meditations* or *The Meditations* was introduced by later editors. It fits quite well because the text contains a series of passages largely consisting of Marcus Aurelius' personal reflections on life, written from the perspective of Stoic philosophy. There are many short aphoristic sayings, but also a few longer passages sometimes showing more rhetorical elegance. The book also contains quotations from earlier philosophers and poets. There are even a few fragments of dialogue, such as this one attributed to Socrates:

> What do you want, souls of rational men or irrational?
> Souls of rational men.
> Of what rational men, sound or unsound?
> Sound.
> Why then do you not seek for them?
> Because we have them.
> Why then do you fight and quarrel? (11.39)

The Codex Palatinus, the Greek manuscript from which Xylander's original printed edition of *The Meditations* derived, bore the title *To Himself*. This is fitting because Marcus is clearly addressing himself throughout and, indeed, he often refers to the notion that he should tell himself various sayings or remind himself of certain philosophical ideas. The first passage of Chapter Two, for instance, opens with the words: "Begin the morning by saying to yourself…" This can be viewed as the beginning of the book proper, in a sense, as it follows what's often viewed as a kind of prologue, in Chapter One. It's one of the most popular passages from the book, so worth quoting:

Begin the morning by saying to yourself, I shall meet with the busy-body, the ungrateful, arrogant, deceitful, envious, unsocial. All these things happen to them by reason of their ignorance of what is good and evil. But I who have seen the nature of the good that it is beautiful, and of the bad that it is ugly, and the nature of him who does wrong, that it is akin to me, not only of the same blood or seed, but that it participates in the same intelligence and the same portion of the divinity, I can neither be injured by any of them, for no one can fix on me what is ugly, nor can I be angry with my kinsman, nor hate him. For we are made for cooperation, like feet, like hands, like eyelids, like the rows of the upper and lower teeth. To act against one another then is contrary to nature; and it is acting against one another to be vexed and to turn away. (2.1)

Structurally, *The Meditations* is divided into twelve chapters or 'books', composed of discrete passages such as this. The number ranges from sixteen to seventy-five per chapter, adding up to 487 passages in total.

There doesn't seem to be a consistent theme for each book that might serve to distinguish it from the others. Book One is the exception. It consists of a series of passages in which Marcus praises his family members and tutors for exhibiting various positive qualities. It's likely that this was intended as a sort of contemplative exercise, whereby he might articulate and try to emulate the virtues exhibited by his loved ones and role models. Later in the text, he provides an explanation for this practice:

When you wish to delight yourself, think of the virtues of those who live with you; for instance, the activity of one, and the modesty of another, and the liberality of a third, and some other good quality of a fourth. For nothing delights so much as the examples of the virtues, when they are exhibited in the morals of those who live with us and present themselves in abundance, as far as is possible. Hence we must keep them before us. (6.48)

Each passage in Book One concentrates on a different person, sixteen individuals in total, except for the closing passage which consists of a brief summary of related blessings for which Marcus thanks the gods.

For the purposes of his own moral and psychological self-improvement, in the rest of *The Meditations* Marcus explores a variety of themes related to Stoic philosophy and its applications in daily life. These mainly relate to justice, death, piety, and overcoming unhealthy desires and emotions. Anger was the emotion with which Marcus was most concerned. In the opening sentence of the book, Marcus praises his grandfather's freedom from anger. Later, he admits that he has struggled to control his own temper sometimes. At one point, Marcus lists ten distinct psychological strategies for overcoming feelings of anger (11.18). He returns to various selections from this list many times throughout *The Meditations*.

LIVING IN AGREEMENT WITH NATURE

Marcus thanks the gods that he knew Apollonius, Rusticus, and Maximus, his three main Stoic tutors, and that he "received clear and frequent impressions about living according to nature, and what kind of a life that is" (1.17). He also says that the Stoic teacher Sextus of Chaeronea, whose lectures he attended later in life, helped him to understand what it meant to "live in accord with Nature" (1.9). This phrase was a well-known slogan, which defines the supreme goal (*telos*) or meaning of life according to Stoic philosophy. Although Marcus never mentions Stoicism by name, he uses this phrase many times throughout *The Meditations*.

"Living in accord with Nature" came to have a double, or even treble, meaning for early Stoics. On the one hand, it means fulfilling our potential by applying reason to the best of our ability in our daily lives – living rationally and *wisely*. For the Stoics, we're both inherently rational and social creatures. Fulfilling our potential therefore requires exercising wisdom in our relationships, whether with individuals or with groups, and to society as a whole.

Wisdom applied to relationships is what the Stoics mean by 'justice'. So living in accord with nature means, in part, living with wisdom and justice. As the virtue of justice (*dikaiosune*) is such a major theme in *The Meditations*, it's worth explaining that the Greek term as used in Stoic philosophy denotes a broader concept than our English word 'justice' tends to suggest. It covers the subordinate virtues of fairness and kindness, and so is expressed in all of our relationships, including how we treat our friends, spouses, and children.

Living in accord with nature, however, has another meaning. It means living in harmony with our fate, not being disturbed or frustrated by the external events that befall us in life. In order to live consistently in accord with wisdom and justice we have to master our fears and desires. Overcoming fear and learning to endure pain and discomfort, when that's our fate, requires the virtue of courage or endurance. Likewise, mastering our desires, so that they're healthy and moderate, requires the virtue of temperance or self-discipline.

The four cardinal virtues of Greek philosophy are wisdom, justice, courage, and temperance. Plato attributes this fourfold schema to Socrates. However, the Stoics employed it more consistently. Living in agreement with nature meant living wisely and virtuously. Diogenes Laertius says that the Stoics defined the supreme goal as a "living according to virtue".

There's therefore both a threefold and fourfold structure in *The Meditations*, derived from early Stoicism. It distinguishes between living harmoniously at three different levels by exercising the four cardinal virtues:

1. **Self**. Wisdom consists in living in harmony with our own true nature as reasoning beings and fulfilling our potential for rationality.
2. **Others**. Justice consists in living in harmony with others, fulfilling our social nature by applying wisdom in a manner designed to build friendships and well-ordered communities.
3. **Nature/Zeus.** The virtues of courage and temperance consist in mastering our fears and desires, respectively, so that we can live in harmony with our fate by accepting events as they befall us. We don't complain or demand more from life than is reasonable and healthy.

As Marcus puts it elsewhere:

There are three relations [between you and other things]: the one to the body which surrounds you; the second to the divine cause from which all things come to all; and the third to those who live with you. (8.27)

The Cynic philosophers believed that virtue is the only true good, vice the only true evil, and that everything else, everything 'external' to our own character and volition, is completely indifferent. One of the key differences between Stoicism and Cynicism was that the Stoics did not view all external things as *equally* indifferent but classed some as 'preferred' and others as 'dispreferred' externals. For example, health is preferable to sickness, wealth to poverty, having friends to having enemies, and so on. Yet we shouldn't attach so much importance to these things that we become upset about them. External things have some value in Stoicism, but they're relatively unimportant. They don't determine whether our life as a whole is good or bad – only virtue or vice can do that. This was explained by the analogy of a set of scales on which virtue is placed on one side. It doesn't matter how many gold coins, or other externals, we place on one side, it should never be enough to tip the balance against virtue. Although it is rational for us to prefer certain externals over others, the Stoic will never sacrifice virtue for the sake of any of them.

THE PHILOSOPHERS OF THE PORCH – A BRIEF HISTORY OF THE STOICS

It's worth delving into the history of Stoicism to get a sense of the intellectual legacy that Marcus was part of, and that he would build on in *The Meditations.*

The Stoic school of philosophy, which Marcus Aurelius was trained in and followed from his youth, was founded at Athens in 301 BC by a Phoenician merchant called Zeno of Citium.

It's a testimony to the appeal of Stoicism that the ancient school endured for nearly five centuries, until around the time of Marcus' death in AD 180. However, perhaps surprisingly given the popularity of the philosophy during his reign, we hear virtually nothing more about Stoics in the ancient world after this time. Stoicism appears to have been assimilated into Neoplatonism, which was itself gradually superseded by Christianity.

Stoicism's founder, Zeno, made a fortune trading the precious purple dye (*porphura*) manufactured from the fermented innards of the murex sea snail. This dye was known as 'royal' or 'imperial' purple because it was worn by kings and emperors. According to one account, after being shipwrecked near the port of Piraeus, and losing his precious cargo at sea, Zeno made his way to Athens. As a foreign immigrant, he found himself alone and penniless, living like a beggar on the streets.

At some point, Zeno journeyed to the temple of Apollo at Delphi and consulted the famous priestess there, known as the Pythia, asking how he could live the best life. Speaking through his oracle, Apollo pronounced that Zeno should "take on the colour not of dead sea snails but of dead men". We can assume this puzzled him at first. We're told he sat down at a bookseller's stall in Athens and by chance found himself reading the second book of Xenophon's *Memorabilia of Socrates*. This contains Socrates' version of a famous speech composed by the Sophist Prodicus, known as *The Choice of Hercules.* The speech was a powerful exhortation to young men to embrace a life of virtue as opposed to hedonism. Sure enough, after reading it, Zeno leapt to his feet asking where he could find a man like Socrates, who had been executed a few generations earlier. He realized that the oracle meant that he should dye his mind with the wisdom of dead philosophers from previous generations.

The bookseller pointed Zeno toward the Cynic philosopher Crates of Thebes, who happened to be walking past at that moment. So Zeno became a follower of the Cynic school for many years and later studied in the Academic school, run by the followers of Plato. He also studied in the Megarian school, founded by another follower of Socrates, Euclid of Megara. Eventually, though, Zeno decided to found a new school of philosophy. It became known as Stoicism after the *Stoa Poikile* or painted porch, on the edge of the Athenian agora, where Zeno's followers would gather to hear him discourse on philosophy. He was succeeded as head of the school by Cleanthes, who in turn was followed by Chrysippus, one of the most highly regarded intellectuals of the ancient world. Chrysippus, a prolific author, revised the doctrines of Zeno and Cleanthes, adding detailed arguments to defend them. These three are therefore regarded collectively as the original teachers of the Stoic school.

The Stoic school continued to thrive in Athens under the leadership of successive *scholarchs*, as the heads of ancient philosophical schools were known. In 155 BC, Diogenes of Babylon, the fifth scholarch, travelled from Greece to Rome on an ambassadorial mission, along with representatives of the Platonic Academy and the Peripatetic school of Aristotle. These three philosophers caused a sensation, and their visit had a lasting influence on Roman society. A few decades after this, the last scholarch of the Athenian school, Panaetius, became the tutor of the Roman general and statesman, Scipio Amelianus, and a group of his friends, known as the Scipionic Circle.

A few generations later, the Roman statesman Cato the Younger was an important representative of Stoic philosophy, which became associated with republican values when he took a stand against Julius Caesar's autocratic rise to power. Cato was friends with another important Roman politician, Cicero, who, although a follower of Academic philosophy, had studied Stoicism at Athens and was intimately acquainted with its teachings. Whereas Cato wrote nothing, Cicero's extensive writings provide one of our main sources for early Stoicism.

Caesar's victory in the civil war led to the end of the Roman Republic, after he appointed himself dictator. Having no children of his own, he adopted his grand-nephew, Octavian, who went on to become the first Roman emperor, Augustus. Augustus had Stoic tutors, perhaps setting a precedent for subsequent generations of Roman statesmen to align themselves with the philosophy during the imperial period.

Most of the writings of earlier Stoics are lost, so our knowledge of ancient Stoic philosophy comes mainly from three later philosophers of the Roman empire. The first is Seneca the Younger, rhetoric tutor and later speechwriter and political advisor to the emperor Nero, who lived in the first century AD. Many of Seneca's letters and essays discussing Stoicism survive today. Nero's Greek secretary owned a slave called Epictetus, who was later freed. Having studied under another famous Stoic called Musonius Rufus, Epictetus went on to become arguably the most famous teacher of philosophy in the history of Rome. Epictetus wrote nothing, but one of his students, a highly accomplished Roman general and statesman named Arrian, transcribed his discussions with students under the title *The Discourses*. From these was distilled a short handbook containing some of Epictetus' key sayings, the *Enchiridion*.

Epictetus moved from Rome to Greece, where he set up a school. Marcus Aurelius was a child when he died so they almost certainly never met. However, we can assume that Marcus must have been personally acquainted with older men who had studied under Epictetus, probably including some of his own Stoic tutors in Rome. Indeed, Marcus says in *The Meditations* that his main Stoic tutor, Junius Rusticus, gave him a copy of certain notes from the lectures of Epictetus:

> *From Rusticus I received the impression that my character required improvement and discipline… and I am indebted to him for being acquainted with the discourses of Epictetus, which he communicated to me out of his own collection. (1.7)*

Marcus refers to Epictetus more often than to any other philosopher. It seems likely he viewed himself as a student, primarily, of Epictetus' brand of Stoicism. Whereas, originally, we're told there were eight volumes of *The Discourses*, only half of those survive today. However, Marcus attributes sayings to Epictetus not found in the surviving *Discourses*, so it seems likely that he'd also read the ones we're missing. Indeed, for all we know other passages in *The Meditations* may contain unattributed quotes or paraphrases from the lost *Discourses* of Epictetus.

WHEN AND WHERE

It's difficult to know for certain when *The Meditations* was actually written. No specific dates are mentioned in the text, and different parts could have been written at different times in Marcus' life. Still, there are a few clues to be found in the text itself and in the Roman histories and elsewhere. At one point, for instance, Marcus mentions that his adoptive brother, the emperor Lucius Verus, has been dead long enough that it would seem odd for his mistress Pantheia still to be grieving beside his casket (8.37). Given that Lucius died in AD 169, this part of *The Meditations* was presumably written in AD 170 or later. Elsewhere, though, Marcus writes to himself, "you now wait for the time when the child shall come out of your wife's womb" (9.3). His youngest child, Vibia Aurelia Sabina, was born in AD 170, which suggests *this* passage must have been written in that year or earlier.

Although Marcus mentions the death of Lucius and other significant figures in his life, he nowhere mentions the loss of his wife, the Empress Faustina the Younger, and if the passage mentioned above refers to her pregnancy, she clearly must have been alive when he wrote it. Neither does he mention the civil war with Avidius Cassius, which occurred earlier in the year of his wife's death. This might be taken to suggest *The Meditations* was completed prior to these events, which both took place in AD 175. The range of dates we're looking at, AD 170 to 175, therefore happen to correspond broadly with the period of the Roman counter-offensive during the First Marcomannic War. At this time, Marcus was fighting several hostile tribes – chiefly the Marcomanni, Quadi, and Sarmatians – along the northern frontier of the Roman empire, marked by the natural boundary of the River Danube.

The notion that *The Meditations* was written during the course of the First Marcomannic War is supported by two rubrics or headings found in the text, which apparently specify Marcus' location at the time of writing. Between the first and second chapters we find the words "Among the Quadi at the Granua", the name of a tributary that joins the River Danube near the Roman city and military camp at Aquincum, the capital of Lower Pannonia. This is located in modern-day Hungary. A different rubric is found between the second and third chapters, which says simply "This in Carnuntum". Carnuntum was the capital of the Roman province of Upper Pannonia, in modern-day Austria, where another important military camp was located on the banks of the Danube.

The simplest assumption is that the first chapter, which is quite distinct from the rest of the book, was written further east at a later stage of the First Marcomannic War, while Marcus was fighting or negotiating peace with the Quadi across the Danube. The rest of the book was probably written earlier at his military base in Carnuntum. It's possible, however, that some of the text may have been written at a later date, perhaps during the Second Marcomannic War, which began in AD 176 and ended with Marcus' death in AD 180. Recently, an archeological find has provided some related evidence. A funerary stele shows that a member of the emperor's praetorian guard – his personal bodyguard – died at Carnuntum in AD 171. We can therefore infer that Marcus was probably stationed there at this time.

THE IMPACT AND LEGACY OF *THE MEDITATIONS*

The Meditations is one of the most loved self-help and spiritual classics of all time. It has had a profound influence on many different people throughout history, ever since the first printed edition of the Greek manuscript was published in 1558, edited by Wilhelm Xylander.

A few decades later, the Flemish humanist Justus Lipsius founded a movement called 'Neostoicism', which sought to integrate Stoicism with Christianity, inspiring renewed interest in the philosophy among European thinkers. Shortly after this, the first English translation of *The Meditations* was published by Méric Casaubon in 1634.

In the eighteenth century, Frederick the Great modelled himself on Marcus Aurelius. Anthony Ashley-Cooper, 3rd Earl of Shaftesbury, wrote his own version of *The Meditations*, called *The Philosophical Regimen*. And the great economist Adam Smith studied *The Meditations*, referring to Marcus as "the mild, the humane, the benevolent Antoninus", in *The Wealth of Nations* (1776).

The influence of *The Meditations* and Stoicism in general continued to spread throughout the nineteenth and twentieth centuries. However, the practical implications of the philosophy were not fully appreciated until the 1950s when it reached a new audience through the founders of cognitive behavioural therapy, or CBT, which is now the leading evidence-based form of modern psychotherapy. In particular, Albert Ellis, the developer of rational emotive behaviour therapy, the main precursor of CBT, frequently mentioned the influence of Stoicism on his approach to psychotherapy:

This principle, which I have inducted from many psychotherapeutic sessions with scores of patients during the last several years, was originally discovered and stated by the ancient Stoic philosophers, especially Zeno of Citium (the founder of the school),

Chrysippus, Panaetius of Rhodes (who introduced Stoicism into Rome), Cicero [sic.], Seneca, Epictetus, and Marcus Aurelius. The truths of Stoicism were perhaps best set forth by Epictetus, who in the first century A.D. wrote in the Enchiridion: "Men are disturbed not by things, but by the views which they take of them." (Ellis, 1962, p. 54)

Aaron T. Beck, the founder of cognitive behavioural therapy, followed Ellis in attributing the philosophical origins of his approach to Stoicism. Indeed, Stoicism and CBT share the same premise, known as the cognitive model of emotion, which holds that our emotions are largely determined by underlying beliefs. Whereas Ellis tended to quote Epictetus, Beck quoted the same Stoic doctrines from George Long's translation of *The Meditations* in order to illustrate the cognitive model of emotion:

If thou art pained by any external thing, it is not the thing that disturbs thee, but thine own judgment about it. And it is in thy power to wipe out this judgment now. (Marcus Aurelius, quoted in Beck, 1976, p. 263)

What the Stoics intuited about the role of beliefs in the cause and cure of emotional disorders, and verified in their own experience, modern psychologists have confirmed in countless scientific research studies: that by changing our thoughts and attitudes we can potentially change our emotions and alleviate much psychological suffering in our lives.

Partly because of the indirect support it received from research on modern psychotherapy, since the 1950s Stoicism has enjoyed a resurgence in popularity. John Steinbeck's novel *East of Eden* (1954) mentions *The Meditations* as a "tiny volume bound in leather". The Tom Wolfe novel about the Stoicism of Epictetus, *A Man in Full* (1998), also helped to reignite popular interest in Stoicism. Marcus Aurelius has also been depicted on the silver screen. In *The Fall of the Roman Empire*

(1964), he was played by Alec Guinness. However, Ridley Scott's *Gladiator* (2000), which featured Richard Harris as Marcus Aurelius, has done the most to ratchet up interest in him and in *The Meditations.*

Since then, an increasing number of popular books influenced by Stoicism such as Ryan Holiday's *The Obstacle Is the Way* (2014) have appeared. Likewise, a growing number of blog articles and podcasts testify to public interest in Stoicism as a powerful and timeless approach to self-help and self-improvement.

ABOUT THE TRANSLATION

This edition of *The Meditations* is based on the classic translation published in 1862 by the English classical scholar George Long (1800–1879). Long's translation is the subject of the poet and literary critic Matthew Arnold's essay *Marcus Aurelius* (1863).

The man whose thoughts Mr. Long has thus faithfully reproduced, is perhaps the most beautiful figure in history. He is one of those consoling and hope-inspiring marks, which stand forever to remind our weak and easily discouraged race how high human goodness and perseverance have once been carried, and may be carried again. The interest of mankind is peculiarly attracted by examples of signal goodness in high places; for that testimony to the worth of goodness is the most striking which is borne by those to whom all the means of pleasure and self-indulgence lay open, by those who had at their command the kingdoms of the world and the glory of them. Marcus Aurelius was the ruler of the grandest of empires; and he was one of the best of men.

Arnold praises the scholarly "fidelity and accuracy" of Long's translation and for treating "Marcus Aurelius's writings, as he treats all the other remains of Greek and Roman antiquity which he touches, not as a dead and dry matter of learning, but as documents with a side of modern applicability and living interest, and valuable mainly so far as this side in them can be made clear."

However, he does raise a minor complaint against Long because his translation "is not quite idiomatic and simple enough". "Small as these matters appear," says Arnold, "they are important when one has to deal with the general public, and not with a small circle of scholars."

This Capstone Classics edition attempts to make Long's text more accessible to modern readers. I have made minor adjustments designed to simplify and modernize the English, but without affecting its meaning.

Marcus Aurelius

Born AD 121 in Rome, to Marcus Annius Verus, a praetor, and Domitia Lucilla, a noblewoman and heiress. He was raised by his mother and grandfather, after the untimely death of his father when Marcus was probably around three years old.

Rome at this time was ruled by Emperor Hadrian. When Hadrian's heir died, he made Marcus' uncle, Antoninus Pius, his new heir. Antoninus, in turn, adopted Marcus as his heir. He married Antoninus' daughter Faustina in 145.

When Antoninus died during an illness in 161, Marcus became emperor. He immediately requested permission to appoint his adoptive brother, Lucius Verus, as co-emperor in a kind of subordinate capacity. After Lucius' death in 169, Marcus was sole ruler.

Major episodes in Marcus Aurelius' reign include the war against the Parthian Empires (in Mesopotamia), which finally ended in 166, and the Marcomannic Wars against Germanic tribes. He also ruled during the Antonine Plague, which was brought back from campaigns and killed millions of Romans.

When not involved in military matters, Marcus' time was taken up with hearing legal cases and petitions. He was considered knowledgeable on the law and just in his decisions.

Marcus died in 180 in Vindobona, modern-day Vienna, leaving his son Commodus to reign. As Emperor, Commodus was considered a disaster, and so Marcus' death is often considered to mark the end of the *Pax Romana*.

REFERENCES

Arnold, Matthew, 1863. 'Marcus Aurelius' in *Essays in Criticism*. London and Cambridge: Macmillan and Co., 1865.

Beck, A.T., 1976. *Cognitive Therapy & Emotional Disorders*. New York: International University Press.

Ellis, A., 1962. *Reason & Emotion in Psychotherapy*. Secaucus, NJ: Citadel.

ABOUT DONALD ROBERTSON

Donald Robertson is a writer, trainer, and cognitive-behavioural psychotherapist. He specializes in the relationship between ancient philosophy and modern evidence-based psychological therapy. Donald was born in Scotland but now lives in Canada. He's the author of six books on philosophy and psychotherapy, including *Stoicism and the Art of Happiness* (2013) and *How to Think Like a Roman Emperor: The Stoic Philosophy of Marcus Aurelius* (2019).

ABOUT TOM BUTLER-BOWDON

Tom Butler-Bowdon is the author of the bestselling 50 Classics series, which brings the ideas of important books to a wider audience. Titles include *50 Philosophy Classics*, *50 Psychology Classics*, *50 Politics Classics*, *50 Self-Help Classics* and *50 Economics Classics.*

As series editor for the Capstone Classics series, Tom has written Introductions to Plato's *The Republic*, Machiavelli's *The Prince*, Adam Smith's *The Wealth of Nations*, Sun Tzu's *The Art of War*, Lao Tzu's *Tao Te Ching*, and Napoleon Hill's *Think and Grow Rich*.

Tom is a graduate of the London School of Economics and the University of Sydney.

www.Butler-Bowdon.com

THE MEDITATIONS

CONTENTS

BOOK ONE

1. From my grandfather Verus I learned good morals and freedom from anger.

2. From the reputation and memory of my father, modesty and a manly character.

3. From my mother, piety and kindness, and abstinence, not only from evil deeds, but even from evil thoughts; and further, simplicity in my way of living, far removed from the habits of the rich.

4. From my great-grandfather, not to have frequented public schools, and to have had good teachers at home, and to know that on such things a man should spend liberally.

5. From my tutor, to be neither of the green nor of the blue party at the games in the Circus, nor a partisan either of the Parmularius or the Scutarius at the gladiators' fights. I also learned endurance of labour from him, and to have few wants, and to work with my own hands, and not to meddle with other people's affairs, and to be unwilling to listen to slander.

6. From Diognetus, not to busy myself with trivial things, and not to give credit to what was said by miracle-workers and charlatans about incantations and the exorcism of demons and such things; and not to breed quails for fighting, nor to give myself up passionately to such things; and to endure freedom of speech; and to have become intimate with philosophy; and to attend the lectures, first of Bacchius, then of Tandasis and

Marcianus; and to have written dialogues in my youth; and to have desired a plank bed with an animal skin cover, and whatever else of the kind belongs to the Grecian discipline.

7. From Rusticus I received the impression that my character required improvement and therapy; and from him I learned not to be led astray into the emulation of Sophists, nor to write on speculative matters, nor to deliver little moralizing speeches, nor to showing off as a man who practises much discipline, or to perform benevolent acts in order to make a display; and to abstain from rhetoric, and poetry, and fine writing; and not to walk about in the house in my ceremonial attire, nor to do other things of the kind; and to write my letters with simplicity, like the letter which Rusticus wrote from Sinuessa to my mother; and with respect to those who have offended me by words, or done me wrong, to be easily disposed to be pacified and reconciled, as soon as they have shown a readiness to be reconciled; and to read carefully, and not to be satisfied with a superficial understanding of a book; nor hastily to give my assent to those who talk overmuch; and I am indebted to him for being acquainted with the discourses of Epictetus, which he communicated to me out of his own collection.

8. From Apollonius I learned freedom of will and undeviating steadiness of purpose; and to look to nothing else, not even for a moment, except to reason; and to be always the same, in sharp pains, on the occasion of the loss of a child, and in long illness; and to see clearly in a living example that the same man can be both most resolute and yielding, and not irritable in giving instruction; and to have had before my eyes a man who clearly considered his experience and his skill in

expounding philosophical principles as the least of his merits; and from him I learned how to receive what are considered favours from friends, without being either humbled by them or letting them pass unnoticed.

9.   From Sextus, a benevolent disposition, and the example of a family governed in a fatherly manner, and the idea of living conformably to nature; and gravity without affectation, and to look carefully after the interests of friends, and to tolerate ignorant persons, and those who form opinions without consideration: he had the power of readily accommodating himself to all, so that conversation with him was more agreeable than any flattery; and at the same time he was most highly venerated by those who associated with him: and he had the ability both to discover and organize, in an intelligent and methodical way, the principles necessary for life; and he never showed anger or any other passion, but was entirely free from passion, and also most affectionate; and he could express approval without noisy display, and he possessed much knowledge without calling attention to it.

10.   From Alexander the grammarian, to refrain from fault-finding, and not to correct or reproach those who uttered any barbarous or strange-sounding expression or solecism; but adeptly to introduce the very expression which ought to have been used, while replying or giving confirmation, or engaging in an inquiry about the topic itself rather than the word, or by some other tactful means of suggestion.

11.   From Fronto I learned to observe what envy, and duplicity, and hypocrisy are in a tyrant, and that generally those among us who are called Patricians are rather deficient in paternal affection.

12.   From Alexander the Platonist, not to say to anyone frequently or without necessity, or to write in a letter, that I have no time to spare; nor continually to excuse the neglect of duties required by our relation to those with whom we live, by claiming to have more urgent business.

13.   From Catulus, not to be indifferent when a friend finds fault, even if he should find fault without reason, but to try to restore him to his usual disposition; and to be ready to speak well of teachers, as it is reported of Domitius and Athenodotus; and to love my children truly.

14.   From my "brother" Severus, to love my kin, and to love truth, and to love justice; and through him I learned to know Thrasea, Helvidius, Cato, Dio, Brutus; and from him I received the idea of a political state in which there is the same law for all, one administered with regard to equal rights and equal freedom of speech, and the idea of a kingly government which respects most of all the freedom of the governed; I learned from him also consistency and undeviating steadiness in my regard for philosophy; and a disposition to do good, and to give to others readily, and to cherish good hopes, and to believe that I am loved by my friends; and in him I observed no attempt to conceal his opinions with respect to those of whom he disapproved, and that his friends had no need to speculate about what he wished or did not wish, but it was quite plain.

15.   From Maximus I learned self-mastery, and not to be led aside by anything; and cheerfulness in all circumstances, as well as in illness; and a good mixture in of gentleness and dignity in one's character, and to do what was set before me without complaining. I noticed that everybody believed that what he said was what he thought, and that in all that he did he

never had any bad intention; and he never showed amazement and surprise, and was never in a hurry, and never put off doing a thing, nor was perplexed nor dejected, nor did he ever laugh to disguise his vexation, nor, on the other hand, was he ever passionate or suspicious. He was accustomed to perform acts of kindness, and was ready to forgive, and was free from all falsehood; and he gave the appearance of a man who could not be diverted from the right path rather than of a man who had to be set right by others. I observed, too, that no man could ever think that he was looked down upon by Maximus, or ever venture to think himself a better man. He had also the art of being humorous in an agreeable way.

16. In my [adoptive] father [the emperor Antoninus Pius] I observed mildness of temper, and unchangeable resolution in the things which he had determined after due deliberation; and no vanity regarding those things which men call honours; and a love of hard work and perseverance; and readiness to listen to those who had anything to propose for the common good; and undeviating firmness in giving to every man according to his deserts; and knowing from experience when to undertake action vigorously and when to relax. And I observed that he had overcome all passion for boys; and he considered himself no more than any other citizen; and he released his friends from all obligation to dine with him or to attend him when he travelled, and those who had failed to accompany him, by reason of any urgent circumstances, always found him the same. I also observed his habit of careful inquiry in all matters of deliberation, and his persistence, and that he never stopped his investigation through being satisfied with appearances which first present themselves; and that his

disposition was to keep his friends, and not to become quickly tired of them, nor to be extravagant in his displays of affection; and to be satisfied on all occasions, and cheerful; and to anticipate events in the distant future, and to provide for the smallest without display; and immediately to put a stop to popular applause and all flattery; and to be constantly watchful over the things which were necessary for the administration of the empire, and to be a good manager of public expenditure, and patiently to endure the blame which he got for such conduct; and he was neither superstitious with respect to the gods, nor did he court men by gifts or by trying to please them, or by flattering the populace; but he showed sobriety in all things and firmness, and never any mean thoughts or action, nor love of novelty for its own sake. And the things which contributed in any way to life's comfort, and of which fortune gives an abundant supply, he used without arrogance and without apology; so that when he had them, he enjoyed them without affectation, and when he did not have them, he did not desire them. No one could ever say of him that he was either a Sophist or servile or a pedant; but everyone acknowledged him to be a man of maturity and accomplishment, above flattery, able to manage his own and other men's affairs. Besides this, he honoured those who were true philosophers, and he did not reproach those who pretended to be philosophers, nor yet was he easily led by them. He was also natural in conversation, and he made himself agreeable without any offensive affectation. He took appropriate care of his body's health, not like one who is overly-attached to life, nor out of personal vanity, nor yet in a careless way, but so that, through his own attention, he very seldom stood in need of the aid of physicians or of medicine or external treatment. He was most ready to give way without envy to those who possessed any particular ability, such as that of eloquence or knowledge of the law or of morals, or of anything else; and he gave them his help, so that each might enjoy reputation according to his deserts; and he always respected the institutions of his country, without any affectation of doing so. Further, he was not fond of change nor unsteady, but he loved to stay in the same places, and to engage himself in the same activities; and after being seized by his headaches he came back immediately fresh and vigorous to his usual occupations. His secrets were very few and exceptional, and only about public matters; and he showed prudence and economy in the exhibition of public spectacles and the construction of public buildings, his donations to the people, and in such things, for he was a man who looked to what ought to be done, not to the reputation which is obtained by one's acts. He did not bathe at inappropriate hours; he was not fond of constructing buildings, nor fussy about what he ate, nor about the texture and colour of his clothes, nor about the beauty of his slaves. His clothing came from Lorium, his villa on the coast, and from Lanuvium generally. We know how he behaved to the toll-collector at Tusculum who asked his pardon; and such was his behaviour in general. There was in him nothing harsh, nor implacable, nor violent, nor, as one may say, anything carried to the sweating point; but he examined all things individually, as if he had plenty of time, and without confusion, in a methodical way, vigorously and consistently. And that might be said of him which is recorded of Socrates, that he was able both to abstain from, and to enjoy, those things which many are too weak to abstain from, and cannot enjoy without excess. But to be strong enough both to bear the one and to be sober in the other is the mark of a man who has a perfect and invincible soul, such as he showed in the illness of Maximus.

17.   To the gods I am indebted for having good grandfathers, good parents, a good sister, good teachers, good associates, good kinsmen and friends, nearly everything good. Further, I owe it to the gods that I did not rush into any offence against any of them, though I had a tendency which, if the opportunity had arisen, might have led me to do something of this kind; but, through their favour, there never was a set of circumstances which might put me to the test. Further, I am thankful to the gods that I was not brought up with my grandfather's concubine any longer than I was, and that I preserved the flower of my youth, and that I did not prove my virility before the proper age, but even deferred the time; that I was subjected to a ruler and a father who was able to take away all conceit from me, and to help me to realize that it is possible for a man to live in a palace without wanting either guards or fancy clothing, or torches and statues, and such things for show; but that it is in such a man's power to bring himself very close to the lifestyle of a private citizen, without being for this reason either meaner in thought, or more remiss in action, with respect to the things which must be done for the public interest in a manner that befits a ruler. I thank the gods for giving me such [an adoptive] brother [Lucius Verus], who was able by his moral character to rouse me to vigilance over myself, and who, at the same time, pleased me by his respect and affection; that my children have not been slow nor physically deformed; that I did not become more proficient in rhetoric, poetry, and the

other studies, in which I should perhaps have been completely engaged if I had seen that I was making progress; that I made haste to place those [teachers] who brought me up in positions of honour, which they seemed to desire, without putting them off with hope of my doing it some time after, because they were then still young; that I knew Apollonius, Rusticus, Maximus; that I received clear and frequent impressions about living according to nature, and what kind of a life that is, so that, so far as depended on the gods, and their gifts, and help, and inspirations, nothing hindered me from forthwith living according to nature, though I still fall short of it through my own fault, and through not observing the admonitions of the gods, and, I may almost say, their direct instructions; that my body has held out so long in such a kind of life; that I never touched either Benedicta or Theodotus, and that, after having fallen into lustful passions, I was cured; and, though I was often irritated with Rusticus, I never did anything of which I needed to repent; that, though it was my mother's fate to die young, she spent the last years of her life with me; that, whenever I wished to help any man in his need, or on any other occasion, I was never told that I had not the means of doing it; and that I never found myself needing to receive such assistance from another; that I have such a wife, so obedient, and so affectionate, and so straightforward; that I had abundance of good tutors for my children; and that remedies have been shown to me by dreams, both others, and against spitting blood and giddiness...; and that, when I had an inclination to philosophy, I did not fall into the hands of any Sophist, and that I did not waste my time on writers of histories, or in resolving logical syllogisms, or occupy myself about the investigation of appearances in the heavens; for all these things require the help of the gods and fortune.

Among the Quadi at the River Granua.

BOOK TWO

1. Begin the morning by saying to yourself, I shall meet with the busybody, the ungrateful, arrogant, deceitful, envious, unsocial. All these things happen to them because of their ignorance of what is good and evil. But I who have seen that the nature of the good is beautiful, and that the bad is ugly, and that the nature of he who does wrong is akin to me, not only of the same blood or seed, but that it participates in the same intelligence and the same portion of the divinity, I can neither be injured by any of them, for no one can fix on me what is ugly, nor can I be angry with my kinsman, nor hate him. For we are made for cooperation, like feet, like hands, like eyelids, like the rows of the upper and lower teeth. To act against one another then is contrary to nature and it is acting against one another to become frustrated and to turn away.

2. Whatever this is that I am, it is a little flesh and breath, and the ruling part. Throw away your books; no longer distract yourself: it is not allowed. But as if you were now dying, despise the flesh. It is blood and bones and a network of nerves, veins, and arteries woven together. See the breath also, what kind of a thing it is, air, and not always the same, but every moment sent out and again sucked in. The third then is the ruling part: consider thus: You are an old man so no longer let this be a slave, no longer be pulled by the strings like a puppet to unsocial

movements, no longer either be dissatisfied with your present lot, or shrink from the future.

3.   All that is from the gods is full of Providence. That which is from fortune is not separated from nature or without an interweaving and involution with the things which are ordered by Providence. From thence all things flow and there is besides necessity, and that which is for the advantage of the whole universe, of which you are a part. But something is good for every part of nature if brought by the nature of the whole, and what serves to maintain this nature. Now the universe is preserved, by the changes of things compounded of the elements as by the changes of the elements themselves. Let these principles be enough for you, let them always be fixed opinions. But cast away your thirst for books, so that you may not die murmuring, but cheerfully, truly, and from your heart thankful to the gods.

4.   Remember how long you have been putting off these things, and how often you have received an opportunity from the gods, and yet do not use it. You must now at last perceive of what universe you are a part, and of what administrator of the universe your existence is an outflowing, and that a limit of time is fixed for you, and if you do not use it for clearing away the clouds from your mind, it will go and you will go with it, and it will never return.

5.   Every moment think steadily as a Roman and a man to do what you have in hand with perfect and simple dignity, and feeling of affection, and freedom, and justice, and to give yourself relief from all other thoughts. And you will give yourself relief, if you do every act of your life as if it were the last, laying aside all carelessness and passionate aversion from the

commands of reason, and all hypocrisy, and self-love, and discontent with the portion which has been given to you. You see how few are the things which if a man lays hold of them, he is able to live a life which flows in quiet and is like the existence of the gods. Because the gods for their part will require nothing more from him who observes these things.

6. Do wrong to yourself, do wrong to yourself, my soul; but you will no longer have the opportunity of honouring yourself. Every man's life is sufficient. But yours is nearly finished, though your soul does not yet revere itself but places its happiness in the souls of others.

7. Do the things external which fall upon you distract you? Give yourself time to learn something new and good, and cease to be whirled around. But then you must also avoid being carried about the other way. For those too are triflers who have wearied themselves in life by their activity, and yet have no object to which to direct every movement, and, in a word, all their thoughts.

8. Through not observing what is in the mind of another a man has seldom been seen to be unhappy but those who do not observe the movements of their own minds must necessarily be unhappy.

9. You must always bear this in mind: what is the nature of the whole, and what is my nature, and how this is related to that, and what kind of a part it is of what kind of a whole, and that there is no-one who hinders you from always doing and saying the things which are according to the nature of which you are a part.

10. Theophrastus, in his comparison of bad acts – such a comparison as one would make in accordance with the

common notions of mankind – says, like a true philosopher, that the offences which are committed through desire are more blameable than those which are committed through anger. For someone who is excited by anger seems to turn away from reason with a certain pain and unconscious contraction but someone who offends through desire, being overpowered by pleasure, seems to be, in a sense, more intemperate and more womanish in his offences. Rightly then, and in a way worthy of philosophy, he said that an offence which is committed with pleasure is more blameable than one which is committed with pain. On the whole, one is more like a person who has been first wronged and through pain is compelled to be angry whereas the other is moved by his own impulse to do wrong, being carried towards doing something by desire.

11.   Since it is possible that you may depart from life this very moment, regulate every act and thought accordingly. But if there are gods, going away from among men is not a thing of which to be afraid because the gods will not involve you in evil. But if indeed they do not exist, or if they have no concern about human affairs, what is it to me to live in a universe devoid of gods or devoid of Providence? But in truth they do exist, and they do care for human things, and they have put all the means in man's power to enable him not to fall into real evils. And as to the rest, if there was anything evil, they would have provided for this also, that it should be altogether in a man's power not to fall into it. Now how can that which does not make a man worse make a man's life worse? But neither through ignorance nor having the knowledge but not the power to guard against or correct these things is it possible that the nature of the universe has overlooked them. Nor is it possible that it has made

so great a mistake, either through want of power or want of skill, that good and evil should happen indiscriminately to the good and the bad. But death certainly, and life, honour and dishonour, pain and pleasure, all these things equally happen to good men and bad, being things which make us neither better nor worse. Therefore they are neither good nor evil.

12. How quickly all things disappear, in the universe the bodies themselves, but in time the memory of them. What is the nature of all sensible things, and particularly those which attract with the bait of pleasure or terrify by pain, or are widely proclaimed by empty fame. How worthless, and contemptible, and sordid, and perishable, and dead they are. All this it is the part of the intellectual faculty to observe. To observe too who these are whose opinions and voices give reputation. What death is, and the fact that, if a man looks at it in itself, and by the abstractive power of reflection resolves into their parts all the things which present themselves to the imagination in it, he will then consider it to be nothing else than an operation of nature. And if anyone is afraid of an operation of nature, he is a child. This, however, is not only an operation of nature, but it is also a thing conducive to the purposes of nature. To observe too how man comes near to the deity, and by what part of him, and when this part of man is so disposed.

13. Nothing is more wretched than a man who traverses everything in a round, and pries into the things beneath the earth, as the poet says, and seeks by conjecture what is in the minds of his neighbours, without perceiving that it is sufficient to attend to the daemon within him, and to revere it sincerely. And reverence of the daemon consists in keeping

it pure from passion and thoughtlessness, and dissatisfaction with what comes from gods and men. For the things from the gods merit veneration for their excellence, and the things from men should be dear to us by reason of kinship. Sometimes even, in a manner, they move our pity by reason of men's ignorance of good and bad, this defect being not less severe than that which deprives us of the power of distinguishing things that are white from things that are black.

14.   Even if you should live three thousand years, and as many times ten thousand years, still remember that no man loses any other life than this which he now lives, nor lives any other than this which he now loses. The longest and shortest are thereby brought to the same. For the present is the same to all, though that which perishes is not the same; and so that which is lost appears to be a mere moment. For a man cannot lose either the past or the future: for what a man has not, how can anyone take this from him? These two things then you must bear in mind; the one, that all things from eternity are of like forms and come round in a circle, and that it makes no difference whether a man shall see the same things during a hundred years or two hundred, or an infinite time; and the second, that the one who lives longest and the one who will die soonest lose just the same. For the present is the only thing of which a man can be deprived, if it is true that this is the only thing which he has, and that a man cannot lose a thing if he has it not.

15.   Remember that all is opinion. For what was said by the Cynic Monimus is manifest: and manifest too is the use of what was said, if a man receives what may be got out of it as far as it is true.

16. The soul of man does violence to itself, first of all, when it becomes an abscess and, as it were, a tumour on the universe, so far as it can. For to be vexed at anything which happens is a separation of ourselves from nature, in some part of which the natures of all other things are contained. In the next place, the soul does violence to itself when it turns away from any man, or even moves towards him with the intention of injuring, such as are the souls of those who are angry. In the third place, the soul does violence to itself when it is overpowered by pleasure or by pain. Fourthly, when it plays a part, and does or says anything insincerely and untruly. Fifthly, when it allows any act of its own and any movement to be without an aim, and does anything thoughtlessly and without considering what it is, it being right that even the smallest things be done with reference to an end. And the end of rational animals is to follow the reason and the law of the most ancient city and political state.

17. Of human life the duration is a point, and the substance is in a flux, and the perception dull, and the composition of the whole body subject to putrefaction, and the soul a whirl, and fortune hard to divine, and fame a thing devoid of judgement. And, to say all in a word, everything which belongs to the body is a stream, and what belongs to the soul is a dream and vapour, and life is a warfare and a stranger's sojourn, and after-fame is oblivion. What then is that which is able to conduct a man? One thing and only one, philosophy. But this consists in keeping the daemon within a man free from violence and unharmed, superior to pains and pleasures, doing nothing without purpose, nor falsely and with hypocrisy, not feeling a need for others to do or not do anything. And besides,

accepting all that happens, and all that is allotted, as coming from there, wherever it is, from whence he himself came. And, finally, waiting for death with a cheerful mind, as being nothing else than a dissolution of the elements of which every living being is compounded. But if there is no harm to the elements themselves in each continually changing into another, why should a man have any apprehension about the change and dissolution of all the elements? For it is according to nature, and nothing is evil which is according to nature.

This in Carnuntum.

BOOK THREE

1.   We ought to consider not only that our life is wasting away daily and that a small part of it is left but another thing also must be taken into account. If a man should live longer, it is quite uncertain whether his understanding will still continue to be sufficient for the comprehension of things, and retain the faculty of contemplation which strives to acquire the knowledge of the divine and the human. For if he shall begin to fall into dotage, perspiration and nutrition and imagination and appetite, and whatever else there is of the kind, will not fail. But the power of making use of ourselves, and filling up the measure of our duty, and clearly separating all appearances, and considering whether a man should now depart from life, and whatever else of the kind absolutely requires a disciplined reason, all this is already extinguished. We must make haste then, not only because we are daily nearer to death, but also because the conception of things and the understanding of them cease first.

2.   We ought to observe also that even the consequences of things which are produced according to nature contain something pleasing and attractive. For instance, when bread is baked some parts are split at the surface, and these parts which thus open, and have a certain fashion contrary to the purpose of the baker's art, are beautiful in a manner, and in a peculiar way excite a desire for eating. And again, figs, when

they are quite ripe, gape open; and in the ripe olives the very circumstance of their being near to rottenness adds a peculiar beauty to the fruit. And the ears of corn bending down, and the lion's eyebrows, and the foam which flows from the mouth of wild boars, and many other things – though they are far from being beautiful, if a man should examine them individually – still, because they are consequent upon the things which are formed by nature, help to adorn them, and they please the mind. So that if a man should have a feeling and deeper insight with respect to the things which are produced in the universe, there is hardly one of those which follow by way of consequence which will not seem to him to be in a manner disposed so as to give pleasure. And so he will see even the real gaping jaws of wild beasts with no less pleasure than those which painters and sculptors show by imitation, and in an old woman and an old man he will be able to see a certain maturity and comeliness, and the attractive loveliness of young persons he will be able to look on with chaste eyes. And many such things will present themselves, not pleasing to every man, but only to one who has become truly familiar with nature and her works.

3.   Hippocrates after curing many diseases himself fell sick and died. The Chaldaeans foretold the deaths of many, and then fate caught them too. Alexander [the Great], Pompey [the Great], and [Julius] Caesar, after so often completely destroying whole cities, and in battle cutting to pieces many ten thousands of cavalry and infantry, themselves too at last departed from life. Heraclitus, after so many speculations on the conflagration of the universe, was filled with water

internally and died smeared all over with mud. Lice destroyed Democritus, and other lice killed Socrates. What does all of this mean? You have embarked, you have made the voyage, you have come to shore. Get out. If indeed to another life, there is no want of gods, not even there. But if to a state without sensation, you will cease to be held by pains and pleasures, and to be a slave to the bodily vessel, which is as much inferior as that which serves it is superior: for the one is intelligence and deity, the other is earth and corruption.

4. Do not waste the remainder of your life in thoughts about others, when you do not refer your thoughts to some object of common utility. For you lose the opportunity to do something else when you have such thoughts as these. What is such a person doing, and why, and what is he saying, and what is he thinking of, and what is he contriving, and whatever else of the kind makes us wander away from the observation of our own ruling power. We ought then to check in the series of our thoughts everything that is without a purpose and useless, but most of all the over-curious feeling and the malignant. And a man should use himself to think of those things only about which if one should suddenly ask, "What have you now in your thoughts?" With perfect openness you might, immediately answer, "This or That". So that from your words it should be plain that everything in you is simple and benevolent, and such as befits a social animal, and one that cares not for thoughts about pleasure or sensual enjoyments at all, nor has any rivalry or envy and suspicion, or anything else for which you would blush if you should say that you had it in your mind. For the man who is such and no longer delays

being among the number of the best, is like a priest and minister of the gods, using too the deity which is planted within him, which makes the man uncontaminated by pleasure, unharmed by any pain, untouched by any insult, feeling no wrong, a fighter in the noblest fight, one who cannot be overpowered by any passion, dyed deep with justice, accepting with all his soul everything which happens and is assigned to him as his portion. And not often, nor yet without great necessity and for the general interest, imagining what another says, or does, or thinks. For it is only what belongs to himself that he makes the matter for his activity. And he constantly thinks of that which is allotted to himself out of the sum total of things, and he makes his own acts fair, and he is persuaded that his own portion is good. For the lot which is assigned to each man is carried along with him and carries him along with it. And he remembers also that every rational animal is his kinsman, and that to care for all men is according to man's nature; and a man should hold on to the opinion not of all, but of those only who confessedly live according to nature. But as to those who do not live so, he always bears in mind what kind of men they are both at home and abroad, both by night and by day, and what they are, and with what men they live an impure life. Accordingly, he does not value at all the praise which comes from such men, since they are not even satisfied with themselves.

5. Do not labour unwillingly or without regard to the common interest, or without due consideration, or with distraction. Do not let studied ornament set off your thoughts, and be neither a man of many words nor busy about too many things. And further, let the deity which is in you be the

guardian of a living being, manly and of ripe age, and engaged in political matters, and a Roman, and a ruler, who has taken his post like a man waiting for the signal which summons him from life, and ready to go, having need neither of oath nor of any man's testimony. Be cheerful also, and do not seek external help or the tranquillity which others give. A man then must stand erect, not be kept erect by others.

6. If you find in human life anything better than justice, truth, temperance, fortitude, and, in a word, anything better than your own mind's self-satisfaction in the things which it enables you to do according to right reason, and in the condition that is assigned to you without your own choice; if, I say, you see anything better than this, turn to it with all your soul, and enjoy that which you hast found to be the best. But if nothing appears to be better than the deity which is planted in you, which has subjected to itself all your appetites, and carefully examines all the impressions, and, as Socrates said, has detached itself from the persuasions of sense, and has submitted itself to the gods, and cares for mankind; if you find everything else smaller and of less value than this, give place to nothing else. For if you once diverge and incline toward it, you will no longer be able to give preference to that good thing which is your proper possession and your own without distraction. For it is not right that anything of any other kind, such as praise from the many, or power, or enjoyment of pleasure, should come into competition with that which is rationally and politically or practically good. All these things, even though they may seem to adapt themselves to the better things in a small degree, obtain the superiority all at once, and carry us

away. But you should, I say, choose the better simply and freely, and hold to it. – But that which is useful is the better. – Well then, if it is useful to you as a rational being, keep to it but if it is only useful to you as an animal, say so, and maintain your judgement without arrogance: only take care that you make the inquiry by a sure method.

7.   Never value anything as profitable to yourself which shall compel you to break your promise, to lose your self-respect, to hate any man, to suspect, to curse, to behave hypocritically, to desire anything which needs walls and curtains. For he who has preferred to everything intelligence and his inner daemon and the worship of its excellence, acts no tragic part, does not groan, will need neither solitude nor much company. And, what is chief of all, he will live without either pursuing or flying from death but whether for a longer or a shorter time he shall have the soul inclosed in the body, he cares not at all. For even if he must depart immediately, he will go as readily as if he were going to do anything else which can be done with decency and order, taking care of this only all through life, that his thoughts turn not away from anything which belongs to an intelligent animal and a member of a civil community.

8.   In the mind of one who is chastened and purified you will find no corrupt matter, nor impurity, nor any sore skinned over. Nor is his life incomplete when fate overtakes him, as one may say of an actor who leaves the stage before ending and finishing the play. Besides, there is in him nothing servile, nor affected, nor too closely bound to other things, nor yet detached from other things, nothing worthy of blame, nothing which seeks a hiding-place.

9.   Revere the faculty which produces opinion. On this faculty it entirely depends whether there shall exist in your ruling part any opinion inconsistent with nature and the constitution of the rational animal. And this faculty promises freedom from hasty judgement, and friendship towards men, and obedience to the gods.

10.   Throwing away then all things, hold to these only which are few and besides bear in mind that every man lives only this present time, which is an indivisible point, and that all the rest of his life is either past or it is uncertain. Short then is the time which every man lives, and small the nook of the earth where he lives and short too the longest posthumous fame. Even this only continues through a succession of poor human beings, who will very soon die, and who do not even know themselves, much less one who died long ago.

11.   To the aids which have been mentioned let this one be added: Make for yourself a definition or description of the thing which is presented to you, so as to see distinctly what kind of a thing it is in its substance, in its nakedness, in its entirety. And tell yourself its proper name, and the names of the things of which it has been compounded, and into which it will be resolved. For nothing so produces elevation of mind as to be able to examine methodically and truly every object which is presented to you in life. And always to look at things so as to see at the same time what kind of universe this is, and what kind of use everything performs in it. And what value everything has with reference to the whole, and what with reference to man, who is a citizen of the highest city, of which all other cities are like families, what each thing is, and of what it is composed, and how long it is the nature of this thing to endure

which now makes an impression on me. And what virtue I have need of with respect to it, such as gentleness, manliness, truth, fidelity, simplicity, contentment, and the rest. Hence, on every occasion a man should say: this comes from God, and this is according to the apportionment and spinning of the thread of destiny, and such coincidence and chance, and this is from one of the same stock, and a kinsman and partner, one who knows not however what is according to his nature. But I know and for this reason I behave towards him according to the natural law of fellowship with benevolence and justice. At the same time however in things indifferent I attempt to ascertain the value of each.

12. If you work at what is before you, following right reason seriously, vigorously, calmly, without allowing anything else to distract you, but keeping your divine part pure, as if you should be bound to give it back immediately. If you hold to this, expecting nothing, fearing nothing, but satisfied with your present activity according to nature, and with heroic truth in every word and sound which you utter, you will live happily. And there is no man who is able to prevent this.

13. Just as physicians always have their instruments and knives ready for cases which suddenly require their skill, so you should have principles ready for understanding things divine and human, and for doing everything, even the smallest, with a recollection of the bond which unites the divine and human to one another. For you will neither do anything well which pertains to man without at the same time having a reference to things divine nor the other way around.

14.   Wander aimlessly no longer. For neither will you read your own memoirs, nor the acts of the ancient Romans and Greeks, and the selections from books which you were reserving for your old age. Hasten then to the end which you have before you, and throwing away idle hopes, come to your own aid while it is in your power to do so, if you care at all for yourself.

15.   They do not know how many things are signified by the words "stealing", "sowing", "buying", "keeping quiet", "seeing what ought to be done". For this is not brought about by the eyes, but by another kind of vision.

16.   Body, soul, intelligence: to the body belong sensations, to the soul appetites, to the intelligence principles. To receive the impressions of forms by means of appearances belongs even to animals. To be pulled by the strings of desire belongs both to wild beasts and to men who have made themselves into women, and to a Phalaris and a Nero. And to have the intelligence that guides to the things which appear suitable belongs also to those who do not believe in the gods, and who betray their country, and do their impure deeds when they have shut the doors. If then everything else is common to all that I have mentioned, there remains that which is peculiar to the good man, to be pleased and content with what happens, and with the thread which is spun for him. And not to defile the divinity which is planted in his breast, nor disturb it by a crowd of images, but to preserve it in tranquillity, following it obediently as a god, neither saying anything contrary to the truth nor doing anything contrary to justice. And if all men refuse to believe that he lives a simple, modest, and contented

life, he is neither angry with any of them, nor does he deviate from the way which leads to the end of life, to which a man ought to come pure, tranquil, ready to depart, and perfectly reconciled to his fate without any compulsion.

BOOK FOUR

1. That which rules within, when it is according to nature, is so affected with respect to the events which happened, that it always easily adapts itself to that which is possible and is presented to it. For it requires no definite material, but it moves towards its purpose, under certain conditions. And it makes a material for itself out of that which opposes it, as fire lays hold of what falls into it, by which a small light would have been extinguished but when the fire is strong, it soon appropriates to itself the matter which is heaped on it, and consumes it, rising higher by means of this very material.

2. Let no act be done without a purpose, nor otherwise than according to the perfect principles of art.

3. Men seek retreats for themselves, houses in the country, seashores, and mountains, and you also tend to desire such things very much. But this is altogether a mark of the most common sort of men, for it is in your power to retire into yourself whenever you shall choose. For nowhere either with more quiet or more freedom from trouble does a man retire than into his own soul, particularly when he has within him such thoughts that by looking into them he is immediately in perfect tranquillity. And I affirm that tranquillity is nothing else than the good ordering of the mind. Constantly give yourself this retreat then, renew yourself, and let your principles be brief and fundamental, which as soon as you shalt recur

to them will be sufficient to cleanse the soul completely and send you back free from all discontent with the things to which you return. For with what are you discontented? With the badness of men? Recall to your mind this conclusion: that rational animals exist for one another, and that to endure is a part of justice, and that men do wrong involuntarily; and consider how many already, after mutual enmity, suspicion, hatred, and fighting, have been stretched dead, reduced to ashes; and be quiet at last. – But perhaps you are dissatisfied with that which is assigned to you out of the universe. – Recall this alternative: either there is providence or [random] atoms, or remember the arguments by which it has been proved that the world is a kind of political community [and be quiet at last]. – But perhaps corporeal things will still fasten upon you. – Then consider also that the mind does not mingle with the breath, whether moving gently or violently, when it has once drawn itself apart and discovered its own power, and think also of all that you have heard and assented to about pain and pleasure [and be quiet at last]. – But perhaps the desire of that thing called fame will torment you. – See how soon everything is forgotten, and look at the chaos of infinite time on each side of [the present], and the emptiness of applause, and the changeableness and want of judgment in those who pretend to give praise, and the narrowness of the space within which it is circumscribed [and be quiet at last]. For the whole earth is a point, and how small a nook in it is this your dwelling, and how few are there in it, and what kind of people are they who will praise you.

This then remains: Remember to retire into this little territory of your own, and above all do not distract or strain yourself, but be free, and look at things as a man, as a human being, as a citizen, as a mortal. But among the things readiest to your hand to which you shalt turn, let there be these two. One is that things do not touch the soul, for they are external and remain immovable; but our perturbations come only from the opinion which is within. The other is that all these things, which you see, change immediately and will no longer be, and constantly bear in mind how many of these changes you have already witnessed. The universe is transformation; life is opinion.

4. If our intellectual part is common, the reason also, in respect of which we are rational beings, is common. If this is so, the reason which commands us what to do, and what not to do, is also common. If this is so, there is a common law also. If this is so, we are fellow-citizens. If this is so, we are members of some political community. If this is so, the world is in a manner a political state. For of what other common political community will anyone say that the whole human race are members? And from there, from this common political community, comes also our very intellectual faculty and reasoning faculty and our capacity for law or else from where do they come? For as my earthly part is a portion given to me from certain earth, and that which is watery from another element, and that which is hot and fiery from some peculiar source (for nothing comes out of that which is nothing, as nothing also returns to non-existence), so also the intellectual part comes from some source.

5. Death is such as generation is, a mystery of nature; composition out of the same elements, and a decomposition into the same; and altogether not a thing of which any man

should be ashamed, for it is not contrary to [the nature of] a reasonable animal, and not contrary to the reason of our constitution.

6. It is natural that these things should be done by such persons, it is a matter of necessity, and if a man will not have it so, he will not allow the fig-tree to have juice. But by all means bear this in mind, that within a very short time both you and he will be dead, and soon not even your names will be left behind.

7. Take away your opinion, and then there is taken away the complaint: "I have been harmed." Take away the complaint that "I have been harmed" and the harm is taken away.

8. That which does not make a man worse than he was, also does not make his life worse, nor does it harm him either from without or from within.

9. The nature of that which is [universally] useful has been compelled to do this.

10. Consider that everything which happens, happens justly, and if you observe carefully, you will find it to be so. I do not say only with respect to the continuity of the series of things, but with respect to what is just, and as if it were done by one who assigns to each thing its value. Observe then as you have begun and whatever you do, do it in conjunction with being good, and in the sense in which a man is properly understood to be good. Keep to this in every action.

11. Do not have such an opinion of things as he has who does you wrong, or such as he wishes you to have, but look at them as they are in truth.

12. A man should always have these two rules in readiness. The first to do only whatever the reason of the ruling and legislating faculty may suggest for the use of men. The second,

to change your opinion if there is anyone at hand who sets you right and moves you from any opinion. But this change of opinion must proceed only from a certain persuasion, as of what is just or of common advantage and the like, not because it appears pleasant or brings reputation.

13.   Do you have reason? – I have. – Why do you not use it then? For if this does its own work, what else do you wish?

14.   You have existed as a part, you shalt disappear in that which produced you; or rather you shall be received back into its seminal principle by transmutation.

15.   Many grains of frankincense on the same altar: one falls sooner another falls later but it makes no difference.

16.   Within ten days you will seem a god to those to whom you are now a beast and an ape, if you will return to your principles and the worship of reason.

17.   Do not act as if you were going to live ten thousand years. Death hangs over you. While you live, while it is in your power, be good.

18.   How much trouble he avoids who does not look to see what his neighbour says or does or thinks, but only to what he does himself, that it may be just and pure. As Agathon says, do not look round at the depraved morals of others, but run straight along the line without deviating from it.

19.   Someone who has a ferocious desire for posthumous fame does not consider that every one of those who remember him will himself also die very soon. Then again so will those who have succeeded them, until the whole remembrance shall have been extinguished as it is transmitted through men who foolishly admire and perish. But even suppose that those who will remember are immortal, and that the remembrance will

be immortal, what then is this to you? And I say not what is it to the dead, but what is it to the living? What is praise, except indeed so far as it has a certain utility? For you now reject unseasonably the gift of nature, clinging to something else…

20.   Everything which is in any way beautiful is beautiful in itself, and terminates in itself, not having praise as part of itself. A thing is therefore made neither worse nor better by being praised. I affirm this also of the things which are called beautiful by the vulgar, for example, material things and works of art. That which is really beautiful has no need of anything; not more than law, not more than truth, not more than benevolence or modesty. Which of these things is beautiful because it is praised, or spoiled by being blamed? Is such a thing as an emerald made worse than it was, if it is not praised? or gold, ivory, purple, a lyre, a little knife, a flower, a shrub?

21.   If souls continue to exist, how does the air contain them from eternity? – But how does the earth contain the bodies of those who have been buried from time so remote? For as here the mutation of these bodies after a certain amount of time, whatever it may be, and their dissolution, make room for other dead bodies, so the souls which are removed into the air after subsisting for some time are transmuted and diffused, and assume a fiery nature by being received into the seminal intelligence of the universe, and in this way make room for the fresh souls which come to dwell there. And this is the answer which a man might give on the hypothesis of souls continuing to exist. But we must not only think of the number of bodies which are thus buried, but also of the number of animals which are daily eaten by us and the other animals. For what a number is consumed, and thus in a manner buried in the bodies of

those who feed on them! And nevertheless this earth receives them by reason of the changes [of these bodies] into blood, and the transformations into the aerial or the fiery element.

What is the investigation into the truth in this matter? The division into that which is material and that which is the cause of form.

22.   Do not be whirled about, but in every movement have respect to justice, and on the occasion of every impression maintain the faculty of comprehension [or understanding].

23.   Everything harmonizes with me, which is harmonious to you, O Universe. Nothing for me is too early nor too late, which is in due time for you. Everything is fruit to me which your seasons bring, O Nature: from you are all things, in you are all things, to you all things return. The poet says, "Dear city of Cecrops" and will you not say, "Dear city of Zeus"?

24.   "Occupy yourself with few things", says the philosopher, "if you would be tranquil." But consider if it would not be better to say, "Do what is necessary, and whatever the reason of the animal which is naturally social requires, and as it requires." For this brings not only the tranquillity which comes from doing well, but also that which comes from doing few things. For the greatest part of what we say and do being unnecessary, if a man takes this away, he will have more leisure and less uneasiness. Accordingly, on every occasion a man should ask himself, "Is this one of the unnecessary things?" Now a man should take away not only unnecessary acts, but also unnecessary thoughts, for thus superfluous acts will not follow after.

25.   Try how the life of the good man suits you, the life of him who is satisfied with his portion out of the whole, and satisfied with his own just acts and benevolent disposition.

26.   Have you seen those things? Look also at these. Do not disturb yourself. Make yourself all simplicity. Does anyone do wrong? It is to himself that he does the wrong. Has anything happened to you? Well, out of the universe from the beginning everything which happens has been apportioned and spun out to you. In a word, your life is short. You must turn the present to profit by the aid of reason and justice. Be sober in your relaxation.

27.   Either it is a well-arranged universe or a chaos huddled together, but still a universe. But can a certain order subsist in you, and disorder in the All? And this too when all things are so separated and diffused and sympathetic.

28.   A black character, a womanish character, a stubborn character, bestial, childish, animal, stupid, counterfeit, scurrilous, fraudulent, tyrannical.

29.   If he is a stranger to the universe who does not know what is in it, no less is he a stranger who does not know what is going on in it. He is a runaway, who flies from social reason; he is blind, who shuts the eyes of understanding; he is poor, who has need of another, and has not from himself all things which are useful for life. He is an abscess on the universe who withdraws and separates himself from the reason of our common nature through being displeased with the things which happen, for the same nature produces this, and has produced you too: he is a piece rent asunder from the state, who tears, his own soul from that of reasonable animals, which is one.

30.   The one is a philosopher without a tunic, and the other without a book: here is another half naked. "Bread I have not," he says, "and I abide by reason – and I do not get

the means of living out of my learning, and I abide [by my reason]."

31. Love the art, poor as it may be, which you have learned, and be content with it. Pass through the rest of life like one who, with his whole soul, has trusted all that he has to the gods, making yourself neither the tyrant nor the slave of any man.

32. Consider, for example, the times of Vespasian. You will see all these things, people marrying, bringing up children, sick, dying, warring, feasting, trafficking, cultivating the ground, flattering, obstinately arrogant, suspecting, plotting, wishing for some to die, grumbling about the present, loving, heaping up treasure, desiring consulship, kingly power. Well, then, that life of these people no longer exists at all. Again, remove to the times of Trajan. Again, all is the same. Their life too is gone. In like manner view also the other epochs of time and of whole nations, and see how many after great efforts soon fell and were resolved into the elements. But chiefly you should think of those whom you have yourself known distracting themselves about idle things, neglecting to do what was in accordance with their proper constitution, and to hold firmly to this and to be content with it. And in doing this it is necessary to remember that the attention given to everything has its proper value and proportion. For thus you will not be dissatisfied, if you apply yourself to smaller matters no further than is fit.

33. The words which were formerly familiar are now antiquated: so also the names of those who were famed of old, are now in a manner antiquated, Camillus, Caeso, Volesus, Leonnatus, and a little after also Scipio and Cato, then Augustus,

then also Hadrian and Antoninus. For all things soon pass away and become a mere tale, and complete oblivion soon buries them. And I say this of those who have shone in a wondrous way. For the rest, as soon as they have breathed out their breath they are gone, and no man speaks of them. And, to conclude the matter, what is even an eternal remembrance? A mere nothing. What then is that about which we ought to employ our serious pains? This one thing, thoughts just, and acts social, and words which never lie, and a disposition which gladly accepts all that happens, as necessary, as usual, as flowing from a principle and source of the same kind.

34.   Willingly give yourself up to Clotho [one of the fates], allowing her to spin your thread into whatever things she pleases.

35.   Everything is only for a day, both that which remembers and that which is remembered.

36.   Observe constantly that all things take place by change, and accustom yourself to consider that the nature of the universe loves nothing so much as to change the things which are and to make new things like them. For everything that exists is in a manner the seed of that which will be. But you are thinking only of seeds which are cast into the earth or into a womb: but this is a very vulgar notion.

37.   You will soon die, and you are not yet simple, nor free from perturbations, nor without suspicion of being hurt by external things, nor kindly disposed towards all, nor do you yet place wisdom only in acting justly.

38.   Examine men's ruling principles, even those of the wise, what kind of things they avoid, and what kind they pursue.

39. What is evil to you does not subsist in the ruling principle of another; nor yet in any turning and mutation of your corporeal covering. Where is it then? It is in that part of you in which subsists the power of forming opinions about evils. Let this power then not form [such] opinions, and all is well. And if that which is nearest to it, the poor body, is cut, burnt, filled with matter and rottenness, nevertheless let the part which forms opinions about these things be quiet. That is, let it judge that nothing is either bad or good which can happen equally to the bad man and the good. For that which happens equally to him who lives contrary to nature and to him who lives according to nature, is neither according to nature nor contrary to nature.

40. Constantly regard the universe as one living being, having one substance and one soul; and observe how all things have reference to one perception, the perception of this one living being; and how all things act with one movement; and how all things are the cooperating causes of all things which exist; observe too the continuous spinning of the thread and the contexture of the web.

41. "You are a little soul bearing about a corpse", as Epictetus used to say.

42. It is no evil for things to undergo change, and no good for things to subsist in consequence of change.

43. Time is like a river made up of the events which happen, and a violent stream. For as soon as a thing has been seen, it is carried away, and another comes in its place, and this will be carried away too.

44. Everything which happens is as familiar and well known as the rose in spring and the fruit in summer for such is

MEDITATIONS

disease, and death, and calumny, and treachery, and whatever else delights fools or vexes them.

45.   In the series of things, those which follow are always aptly fitted to those which have gone before. For this series is not like a mere enumeration of disjointed things, which has only a necessary sequence, but it is a rational connection: and as all existing things are arranged together harmoniously, so the things which come into existence exhibit no mere succession, but a certain wonderful relationship.

46.   Always remember the saying of Heraclitus, that the death of earth is to become water, and the death of water is to become air, and the death of air is to become fire, and reversely. And think too of him who forgets whither the way leads, and that men quarrel with that with which they are most constantly in communion, the reason which governs the universe; and the things which they daily meet with seem to them strange: and consider that we ought not to act and speak as if we were asleep, for even in sleep we seem to act and speak; and that we ought not, like children who learn from their parents, simply to act and speak as we have been taught.

47.   If any god told you that you shall die tomorrow, or certainly on the day after tomorrow, you would not care much whether it was on the third day or on the morrow, unless you were mean-spirited in the highest degree. For how small is the difference! So think it no great thing to die after as many years as you can name rather than tomorrow.

48.   Think continually how many physicians are dead after often contracting their eyebrows over the sick, and how many astrologers after predicting with great pretensions the deaths of others, and how many philosophers after endless

44

discourses on death or immortality, how many heroes after killing thousands, and how many tyrants who have used their power over men's lives with terrible insolence, as if they were immortal. And how many cities are entirely dead, so to speak, Helice and Pompeii and Herculaneum, and others innumerable. Add to the reckoning all whom you have known, one after another. One man after burying another has been laid out dead, and another buries him, and all this in a short time. To conclude, always observe how ephemeral and worthless human things are, and what was yesterday a little mucus, tomorrow will be a mummy or ashes. Pass then through this little space of time conformably to nature, and end your journey in content, as an olive falls off when it is ripe, blessing nature who produced it, and thanking the tree on which it grew.

49.   Be like the promontory against which the waves continually break, but it stands firm and tames the fury of the water around it.

Am I unhappy because this has happened to me? Not so, but rather I am happy, though this has happened to me, because I continue free from pain, neither crushed by the present nor fearing the future. For such a thing as this might have happened to every man but every man would not have continued free from pain on such an occasion. Why then is that rather a misfortune than this a good fortune? And do you in all cases call that a man's misfortune which is not a deviation from man's nature? And does a thing seem to you to be a deviation from man's nature, when it is not contrary to the will of man's nature? Well, you know the will of nature. Will then this which has happened prevent you from being just, magnanimous, temperate, prudent, secure against inconsiderate opinions and falsehood? Will it prevent you from having modesty, freedom, and everything else, by the presence of which man's nature obtains all that is its own? Remember too on every occasion which leads you to vexation to apply this principle: not that this is a misfortune, but that to bear it nobly is good fortune.

50.   It is a vulgar, but still a useful help towards contempt of death, to pass in review those who have tenaciously clung to life. What more then have they gained than those who have died early? Certainly they lie in their tombs somewhere at last, Cadicianus, Fabius, Julianus, Lepidus, or anyone else like them, who have carried out many to be buried, and then were carried out themselves. Altogether the interval is small [between birth and death] and consider with how much trouble, and in company with what sort of people, and in what a feeble body, this interval is laboriously passed. Do not then consider life a thing of any value. For look to the immensity of time behind you, and to the time which is before you, another boundless space. In this infinity then what is the difference between him who lives three days and him who lives three generations?

51.   Always run to the short way; and the short way is the natural: accordingly say and do everything in conformity with the soundest reason. For such a purpose frees a man from trouble, and warfare, and all artifice and ostentatious display.

BOOK FIVE

1. In the morning when you rise reluctantly, let this thought be present: I am rising to do the work of a human being. Why then am I dissatisfied if I am going to do the things for which I exist and for which I was brought into the world? Or have I been made for this, to lie in the bedclothes and keep myself warm? – But this is more pleasant. – Do you exist then to take your pleasure and not at all for action or exertion? Do you not see the little plants, the little birds, the ants, the spiders, the bees working together to put in order their various parts of the universe? And are you unwilling to do the work of a human being, and do you not make haste to do that which is according to your nature? – But it is necessary to take rest also. – It is necessary. However, Nature has fixed bounds to this too: she has fixed bounds to eating and drinking, and yet you go beyond these bounds, beyond what is sufficient. Yet in your acts it is not so but you stop short of what you can do. So you do not love yourself, for if you did you would love your nature and her will. Those who love their arts exhaust themselves in working at them unwashed and without food but you value your own nature less than the turner values the turning art, or the dancer the dancing art, or the lover of money values his money, or the vainglorious man his little glory. And such men, when they have an emotional attachment to a thing choose neither to eat nor to sleep rather than to perfect the things for which

47

they care. But are the acts which concern society more vile in your eyes and less worthy of your labour?

2.   How easy it is to repel and to wipe away every impression which is troublesome or unsuitable, and immediately to be in all tranquillity.

3.   Judge every word and deed which are according to nature to be fit for you; and be not diverted by the blame which follows from any people, nor by their words, but if a thing is good to be done or said, do not consider it unworthy of you. For those persons have their peculiar leading principle and follow their peculiar movement; which things do not you regard, but go straight on, following your own nature and the common nature; and the way of both is one.

4.   I go through the things which happen according to nature until I shall fall and rest, breathing out my breath into that element out of which I daily draw it in, and falling upon that earth out of which my father collected the seed, and my mother the blood, and my nurse the milk; out of which during so many years I have been supplied with food and drink; which bears me when I tread on it and abuse it for so many purposes.

5.   You say that men cannot admire the sharpness of your wits. – Be it so: but there are many other things of which you cannot say that you are not formed for them by nature. Show those qualities then which are altogether in your power, sincerity, gravity, endurance of labour, aversion to pleasure, contentment with your portion and with few things, benevolence, frankness, no love of superfluity, freedom from trifling, magnanimity. Do you not see how many qualities you are immediately able to exhibit, for which you do not have

the excuse of natural incapacity and unfitness, and yet you still remain voluntarily below the mark? Or are you compelled through being defectively furnished by nature to murmur, and to be stingy, and to flatter, and to find fault with your poor body, and to try to please men, and to make great display, and to be so restless in your mind? No, by the gods, but you might have been delivered from these things long ago. Only if in truth you can be charged with being rather slow and dull of comprehension, you must exert yourself about this also, not neglecting it nor yet taking pleasure in your dullness.

6. One man, when he has done a service to another, is ready to set it down to his account as a favour conferred. Another is not ready to do this, but still in his own mind he thinks of the man as his debtor, and he knows what he has done. A third in a manner does not even know what he has done, but he is like a vine which has produced grapes, and seeks for nothing more after it has once produced its proper fruit. As a horse when he has run, a dog when he has tackled the game, a bee when it has made the honey, so a man when he has done a good act does not call out for others to come and see, but he goes on to another act, as a vine goes on to produce again the grapes in season. – Must a man then, in a sense, act thus without observing it? – Yes. – But this very thing is necessary, the observation of what a man is doing: for, it may be said, it is characteristic of the social animal to perceive that he is working in a social manner, and indeed to wish that his social partner also should perceive it. – It is true what you say, but you do not properly understand what is now said: and for this reason you will become one of those of whom I spoke before, for

even they are misled by a certain show of reason. But if you will choose to understand the meaning of what is said, do not fear that for this reason you will omit any social act.

7. A prayer of the Athenians: "Rain, rain, O dear Zeus, down on the ploughed fields of the Athenians and on the plains." In truth we ought not to pray at all, or we ought to pray in this simple and noble fashion.

8. Just as we must understand when it is said that Asclepius [the god of medicine] prescribed to this man horse-exercise, or bathing in cold water, or going without shoes, so we must understand it when it is said that the nature of the universe prescribed to this man disease, or mutilation, or loss, or anything else of the kind. For in the first case "prescribed" means something like this: "he prescribed this for this man as a thing adapted to procure health." In the second case it means "That which happens to [or suits] every man is fixed in a manner for him suitably to his destiny." For this is what we mean when we say that things are suitable to us, as the workmen say of squared stones in walls or the pyramids, that they are suitable, when they fit them to one another in some kind of connection. For there is altogether one fitness [harmony]. And as the universe is made up out of all bodies to be such a body as it is, so out of all existing causes necessity [destiny] is made up to be such a cause as it is. And even those who are completely ignorant understand what I mean, for they say, "It [necessity, destiny] brought this to such a person." This then was brought and this was prescribed to him. Let us then receive these things, as well as those which Asclepius prescribes. Many as a matter of course even among his prescriptions are disagreeable, but we accept them in the hope of health. Let the perfecting

and accomplishment of the things which the common nature judges to be good, be judged by you to be of the same kind as your health. And so accept everything which happens, even if it seem disagreeable, because it leads to this, to the health of the universe and to the prosperity and happiness of Zeus. For he would not have brought on any man what he has brought, if it were not useful for the whole. Neither does the nature of anything, whatever it may be, cause anything which is not suitable to that which is directed by it. For two reasons then it is right to be content with that which happens to you: the one, because it was done for you and prescribed for you, and in a manner had reference to you, originally from the most ancient causes spun with your destiny, and the other, because even that which comes individually to every man is to the power which administers the universe a cause of happiness and perfection, indeed even of its very continuance. For the integrity of the whole is mutilated, if you cut off anything whatever from the conjunction and the continuity either of the parts or of the causes. And you do cut off, as far as it is in your power, when you are dissatisfied, and in a manner try to put anything out of the way.

9. Do not be disgusted, discouraged, or dissatisfied, if you do not succeed in doing everything according to right principles. Rather when you have failed, return back again, and be content if the greater part of what you do is consistent with man's nature, and love this to which you return. Do not return to philosophy as if she were a master, but act like those who have sore eyes and apply a bit of sponge and egg, or as another applies a plaster, or drenching with water. For thus you will not fail to obey reason, and you will repose in it. And remember that philosophy requires only things which your

nature requires but you would have something else which is not according to nature. It may be objected, "Why, what is more agreeable than this [which I am doing]?" But is not this the very reason why pleasure deceives us? And consider if magnanimity, freedom, simplicity, equanimity, piety, are not more agreeable. For what is more agreeable than wisdom itself, when you think of the security and the happy course of all things which depend on the faculty of understanding and knowledge?

10. Things are in such a kind of envelopment that they have seemed to philosophers, not a few nor those common philosophers, altogether unintelligible. Indeed, they even seem difficult to understand to the Stoics themselves. And all our assent is changeable for where is the man who never changes? Carry your thoughts then to the objects themselves, and consider how short-lived they are and worthless, and that they may be in the possession of a filthy wretch or a whore or a robber. Then turn to the morals of those who live with you, and it is hardly possible to endure even the most agreeable of them, to say nothing of a man being hardly able to endure himself. In such darkness then and dirt, and in so constant a flux both of substance and of time, and of motion and of things moved, what there is worth being highly prized, or even an object of serious pursuit, I cannot imagine. But on the contrary it is a man's duty to comfort himself, and to wait for the natural dissolution, and not to be vexed at the delay, but to rest in these principles only: first, that nothing will happen to me which is not conformable to the nature of the universe and second, that it is in my power never to act contrary to my god and inner daemon for there is no man who will compel me to this.

11.   About what am I now employing my own soul? On every occasion I must ask myself this question, and inquire, "What have I now in this part of me which they call the ruling principle? And whose soul have I now? That of a child, or of a young man, or of a feeble woman, or of a tyrant, or of a domestic animal, or of a wild beast?"

12.   We may learn even from this what kind of things appear good to the many. For if any man should conceive certain things as being really good, such as prudence, temperance, justice, fortitude, he would not after having first conceived these endure to listen to anything which should not be in harmony with what is really good. But if a man has first conceived as good the things which appear to the many to be good, he will listen and readily receive as very applicable that which was said by the comic writer. Thus even the many perceive the difference. For were it not so, this saying would not offend and would not be rejected [in the first case], while we receive it when it is said of wealth, and of the means which further luxury and fame, as said fitly and wittily. Go on then and ask if we should value and think those things to be good, to which after their first conception in the mind the words of the comic writer might be aptly applied: "that he who has them, through pure abundance has not a place in which to relieve himself."

13.   I am composed of the formal and the material. Neither of them will perish into non-existence, as neither of them came into existence out of non-existence. Every part of me then will be reduced by change into some part of the universe, and that again will change into another part of the universe, and so on forever. And by consequence of such a

change I too exist, and those who begot me, and so on forever in the other direction. For nothing hinders us from saying so, even if the universe is administered according to definite periods [of revolution].

14. Reason and the reasoning art [philosophy] are powers which are sufficient for themselves and for their own works. They move then from a first principle which is their own, and they make their way to the end which is proposed to them; and this is the reason why such acts are named Catorthoseis or right acts, which word signifies that they proceed by the right road.

15. None of these things ought to be called a man's, which do not belong to a man, as man. They are not required of a man, nor does man's nature promise them, nor are they the means of man's nature attaining its end. Neither then does the end of man lie in these things, nor yet that which aids to the accomplishment of this end. And that which aids toward this end is that which is good. Besides, if any of these things did belong to man, it would not be right for a man to despise them and to set himself against them. Nor would a man be worthy of praise who showed that he did not want these things, nor would someone be good who stinted himself in any of them if indeed these things were good. But when a man deprives himself of these things, or of other things like them, or even when he is deprived of any of them, he is a better man to the extent that he patiently endures the loss.

16. Such as are your habitual thoughts, so also will be the character of your mind. For the soul is dyed by its thoughts. Dye it then with a continuous series of such thoughts as these: for instance, that where a man can live, there he can also live well. But he must live in a palace – well then, he can also live

well in a palace. And again, consider that for whatever purpose each thing has been constituted, for this it has been constituted, and towards this it is carried and its end is in that towards which it is carried. Where the end is, there also is the advantage and the good of each thing. Now the good for the reasonable animal is society. For it has been shown above that we are made for society. Is it not plain that the inferior exists for the sake of the superior? But the things which have life are superior to those which have not life, and of those which have life the superior are those which have reason.

17.   To seek what is impossible is madness but it is impossible that the bad should not do something of this kind.

18.   Nothing happens to any man which he is not formed by nature to bear. The same things happen to someone else, and either because he does not see that they have happened, or because he would show a great spirit, he is firm and remains unharmed. It is a shame then that ignorance and conceit should be stronger than wisdom.

19.   Things themselves touch not the soul, not in the least degree, nor have they admission to the soul, nor can they turn or move the soul. The soul turns and moves itself alone, and whatever judgments it may think proper to make, such it makes for itself the things which present themselves to it.

20.   In one respect man is the nearest thing to me, so far as I must do good to men and endure them. But so far as some men make themselves obstacles to my proper acts, man becomes to me one of the things which are indifferent, no less than the sun or wind or a wild beast. Now it is true that these may impede my action, but they are no impediments to my affects and disposition, which have the power of acting

conditionally and changing. For the mind converts and changes every hindrance to its activity into an aid. And so that which is a hindrance is made a furtherance to an act and that which is an obstacle on the road helps us on this road.

21.   Revere that which is best in the universe, that which makes use of all things and directs all things. And in this manner also revere that which is best in yourself and this is of the same kind as that. For in yourself also, that which makes use of everything else is this, and your life is directed by this.

22.   That which does no harm to the state does no harm to the citizen. In the case of every appearance of harm apply this rule: if the state is not harmed by this neither am I harmed. But if the state is harmed, you must not be angry with him who does harm to the state. Show him where his error is.

23.   Often think of the rapidity with which things pass by and disappear, both the things which are and the things which are produced. For substance is like a river in a continual flow, and the activities of things are in constant change, and the causes work in infinite varieties; and there is hardly anything which stands still. And consider this which is near to you, this boundless abyss of the past and of the future in which all things disappear. How then is he not a fool who is puffed up with such things or plagued about them and makes himself miserable? For they vex him only for a time, and indeed for a time that is short.

24.   Think of the universal substance, of which you have a very small portion and of universal time, of which a short and indivisible interval has been assigned to you. And of that which is fixed by destiny, and how small a part of it you are.

25.   Does another do me wrong? Let him look to it. He has his own disposition, his own activity. I now have what the universal nature now wills me to have and I do what my nature now wills me to do.

26.   Let the part of your soul which leads and governs be undisturbed by the movements in the flesh, whether of pleasure or of pain. And do not allow it to unite with them but let it circumscribe itself and limit those affects to their parts. But when these affects rise up to the mind by virtue of that other sympathy that naturally exists in a body which is all one, then you must not strive to resist the sensation, for it is natural. But do not allow your ruling part of itself add to the sensation the opinion that it is either good or bad.

27.   Live with the gods. And he does live with the gods who constantly shows to them that his own soul is satisfied with that which is assigned to him, and that it does all that the daemon wishes, which Zeus hath given to every man for his guardian and guide, a portion of himself. And this is every man's understanding and reason.

28.   Are you angry with someone whose armpits stink? Are you angry with one whose breath smells foul? What good will this anger do you? He has such a mouth, he has such armpits: it is necessary that such an emanation must come from such things. But the man has reason, it will be said, and he is able, if he takes pains, to discover the source of his offence. I wish you well of your discovery. Well then, and you have reason. By your rational faculty stir up his rational faculty, show him his error, admonish him. For if he listens, you will cure him, and there is no need of anger.

29.   As you intend to live when they are gone out … so it is in your power to live here. But if men do not permit you, then get away out of life, yet do so as if you wert suffering no harm. The house is smoky, and I quit it. Why do you think that this is any trouble? But so long as nothing of the kind drives me out, I remain, am free, no man shall hinder me from doing what I choose, and I choose to do what is according to the nature of the rational and social animal.

30.   The intelligence of the universe is social. Accordingly it has made the inferior things for the sake of the superior, and it has fitted the superior to one another. You see how it has subordinated, co-ordinated, and assigned to everything its proper portion, and has brought together into concord with one another the things which are the best.

31.   How have you behaved hitherto toward the gods, your parents, brethren, children, teachers, to those who looked after your infancy, to your friends, kinsfolk, to your slaves? Consider if you have hitherto behaved to all in such a way that this may be said of you,—

"Never has wronged a man in deed or word."

And call to recollection both how many things you have passed through, and how many things you have been able to endure, and that the history of your life is now complete and your service is ended. And how many beautiful things you have seen, and how many pleasures and pains you have despised, and how many things called honourable you have spurned, and to how many ill-minded folks you have shown a kind disposition.

32.   Why do unskilled and ignorant souls disturb him who has skill and knowledge? What soul then has skill and

knowledge? That which knows the beginning and the end, and knows the reason which pervades all substance, and though all time by fixed periods [revolutions] administers the universe.

33.   Soon, very soon, you will be ashes, or a skeleton, and either a name or not even a name. But name is sound and echo. And the things which are much valued in life are empty and rotten and trifling, and [like] little dogs biting one another, and little children quarrelling, laughing, and then straightway weeping. But fidelity and modesty and justice and truth are fled.

Up to Olympus from the wide-spread earth. [Hesiod, *Works*, V. 197]

What then is there which still detains you here, if the objects of sense are easily changed and never stand still, and the organs of perception are dull and easily receive false impressions, and the poor soul itself is an exhalation from blood? But to have good repute amid such a world as this is an empty thing. Why then do you not wait in tranquillity for your end, whether it is extinction or removal to another state? And until that time comes, what is sufficient? Why, what else than to venerate the gods and bless them, and to do good to men, and to practise tolerance and self-restraint but as to everything which is beyond the limits of the poor flesh and breath, to remember that this is neither yours nor in your power.

34.   You can pass your life in an equable flow of happiness, if you can go by the right way, and think and act in the right way. These two things are common both to the soul of God and to the soul of man, and to the soul of every rational being: not to be hindered by another, and to hold good to consist in the

disposition to justice and the practice of it, and in this to let your desire find its termination.

35.   If this is neither my own badness, nor an effect of my own badness, and the common good is not injured, why am I troubled about it, and what is the harm to the common good?

36.   Do not be carried along inconsiderately by the appearance of things, but give help [to all] according to your ability and their fitness. And if they should have sustained loss in matters which are indifferent, do not imagine this to be a damage for it is a bad habit. But as the old man, when he went away, asked back his foster-child's top, remembering that it was a top, so do you in this case also.

When you are calling out on the Rostra, have you forgotten, man, what these things are? – Yes but they are objects of great concern to these people – will you too then be made a fool for these things? I was once a fortunate man, but I lost it, I know not how. – But fortunate means that a man has assigned to himself a good fortune, and a good fortune is good disposition of the soul, good emotions, good actions.

BOOK SIX

1.   The substance of the universe is obedient and compliant; and the reason which governs it has in itself no cause for doing evil, for it has no malice, nor does it do evil to anything, nor is anything harmed by it. But all things are made and perfected according to this reason.

2.   Let it make no difference to you whether you are cold or warm, if you are doing your duty. And whether you are drowsy or satisfied with sleep, whether spoken of ill or praised, and whether dying or doing something else. For it is one of the acts of life, this act by which we die, it is sufficient then in this act also to do well what we have in hand.

3.   Look within. Let neither the peculiar quality of anything nor its value escape you.

4.   All existing things soon change, and they will either be reduced to vapour, if indeed all substance is one, or they will be dispersed.

5.   The reason which governs knows what its own disposition is, and what it does, and on what material it works.

6.   The best way of avenging yourself is not to become like [the wrong-doer].

7.   Take pleasure in one thing and rest in it, in passing from one social act to another social act, thinking of God.

8.   The ruling principle is that which rouses and turns itself, and while it makes itself such as it is and such as it wills

to be, it also makes everything which happens appear to itself to be such as it wills.

9. In conformity to the nature of the universe every single thing is accomplished; for certainly it is not in conformity to any other nature that each thing is accomplished, either a nature which externally comprehends this, or a nature which is comprehended within this nature, or a nature external and independent of this.

10. The universe is either a confusion, and a mutual involution of things, and a dispersion, or it is unity and order and providence. If then it is the former, why do I desire to tarry in a fortuitous combination of things and such a disorder? And why do I care about anything else than how I shall at last become earth? And why am I disturbed, for the dispersion of my elements will happen whatever I do? But if the other supposition is true, I venerate, and I am firm, and I trust in him who governs.

11. When you hast been compelled by circumstances to be disturbed in a manner, quickly return to yourself, and do not continue out of tune longer than the compulsion lasts for you will have more mastery over the harmony by continually recurring to it.

12. If you had a stepmother and a mother at the same time, you would be dutiful to your stepmother, but still you would constantly return to your mother. Let the court and philosophy now be to you stepmother and mother. Return to philosophy frequently and repose in her, through her what you meet with in the court appears to you tolerable, and you appear tolerable in court.

13.   When we have meat before us and such eatables, we receive the impression that this is the dead body of a fish, and this the dead body of a bird or of a pig. And again, that this Falernian wine is only a little grape juice, and this purple robe some sheep's wool dyed with the blood of a shellfish. Such then are these impressions, and they reach the things themselves and penetrate them, and so we see what kind of things they are. Just in the same way ought we to act all through life, and where there are things which appear most worthy of our approbation, we ought to lay them bare and look at their worthlessness and strip them of all the words by which they are exalted. For outward show is a wonderful perverter of the reason, and when you are most sure that you are employed about things worth your pains, it is then that it cheats you most. Consider then what Crates says of Xenocrates himself.

14.   Most of the things which the multitude admire are referred to objects of the most general kind, those which are held together by cohesion or natural organization, such as stones, wood, fig trees, vines, olives. But those which are admired by men, who are a little more reasonable, are referred to the things which are held together by a living principle, such as flocks or herds. Those which are admired by men who are still more instructed are the things which are held together by a rational soul, not however a universal soul, but rational so far as it is a soul skilled in some art, or expert in some other way, or simply rational so far as it possesses a number of slaves. But he who values a rational soul, a soul universal and fitted for political life, regards nothing else except this and above all things he keeps his soul in a condition and in an activity

conformable to reason and social life, and he co-operates to this end with those who are of the same kind as himself.

15.   Some things are hurrying into existence, and others are hurrying out of it; and of that which is coming into existence part is already extinguished. Motions and changes are continually renewing the world, just as the uninterrupted course of time is always renewing the infinite duration of ages. In this flowing stream then, on which there is no abiding, what is there of the things which hurry by on which a man would set a high price? It would be just as if a man should fall in love with one of the sparrows which fly by, but it has already passed out of sight. Something of this kind is the very life of every man, like the exhalation of the blood and the respiration of the air. For such as it is to have once drawn in the air and to have given it back, which we do every moment, just the same is it with the whole respiratory power, which you received at your birth yesterday and the day before, to give it back to the element from which you first drew it.

16.   Neither is transpiration, as in plants, a thing to be valued, nor respiration, as in domesticated animals and wild beasts, nor the receiving of impressions by the appearances of things, nor being moved by desires as puppets by strings, nor assembling in herds, nor being nourished by food for this is just like the act of separating and parting with the useless part of our food. What then is worth being valued? To be received with clapping of hands? No. Neither must we value the clapping of tongues; for the praise which comes from the many is a clapping of tongues. Suppose then that you hast given up this worthless thing called fame, what remains that is worth valuing? This, in my opinion: to move yourself and to

restrain yourself in conformity to your proper constitution, to which end both all employments and arts lead. For every art aims at this, that the thing which has been made should be adapted to the work for which it has been made; and both the vine-planter who looks after the vine, and the horse-breaker, and he who trains the dog, seek this end. But the education and the teaching of youth aim at something. In this then is the value of the education and the teaching. And if this is well, you will not seek anything else. will you not cease to value many other things too? Then you will be neither free, nor sufficient for your own happiness, nor without passion. For of necessity you must be envious, jealous, and suspicious of those who can take away those things, and plot against those who have that which is valued by you. Of necessity a man must be altogether in a state of perturbation who wants any of these things; and besides, he must often find fault with the gods. But to revere and honour your own mind will make you content with yourself, and in harmony with society, and in agreement with the gods, that is, praising all that they give and have ordered.

17. Above, below, all around are the movements of the elements. But the motion of virtue is in none of these: it is something more divine, and advancing by a way hardly observed, it goes happily on its road.

18. How strangely men act! They will not praise those who are living at the same time and living with themselves but they set much value on being praised themselves by posterity, by those whom they have never seen nor ever will see. But this is very much the same as if you should be grieved because those who have lived before you did not praise you.

19.   If a thing is difficult to be accomplished by yourself, do not think that it is impossible for man. But if anything is possible for man and conformable to his nature, think that this can be attained by you too.

20.   In the gymnastic [wrestling] exercises suppose that a man has torn you with his nails, and by dashing against your head has inflicted a wound. Well, we neither show any signs of vexation, nor are we offended, nor do we suspect him afterwards as a treacherous fellow; and yet we are on our guard against him, not however as an enemy, nor yet with suspicion, but we quietly get out of his way. Something like this let your behaviour be in all the other parts of life. Let us overlook many things in those who are like antagonists in the gymnasium. For it is in our power, as I said, to get out of the way, and to have no suspicion nor hatred.

21.   If any man is able to convince me and show me that I do not think or act right, I will gladly change; for I seek the truth, by which no man was ever injured. But he is injured who abides in his error and ignorance.

22.   I do my duty, other things trouble me not. For they are either things without life, or things without reason, or things that have rambled and know not the way.

23.   As to the animals which have no reason, and generally all things and objects, make use of them with a generous and liberal spirit, since you have reason and they have none. But towards human beings, as they have reason, behave in a social spirit. And on all occasions call on the gods, and do not perplex yourself about the length of time in which you shall do this for even three hours so spent are sufficient.

24.   Alexander the Great and his groom were brought to the same state by death. For either they were received among the same seminal principles of the universe, or they were alike dispersed among the atoms.

25.   Consider how many things in the same indivisible time take place in each of us – things which concern the body and things which concern the soul. And so you will not wonder if many more things, or rather all things which come into existence in that which is the one and all, which we call Cosmos, exist in it at the same time.

26.   If any man should propose to you the question, how the name Antoninus is written, would you utter each letter with a straining of the voice? What then if they grow angry, will you be angry too? Will you not go on with composure and number every letter? Just so then in this life also remember that every duty is made up of certain parts. These it is your duty to observe, and without being disturbed or showing anger towards those who are angry with you, to go on your way and finish that which is set before you.

27.   How cruel it is not to allow men to strive after the things which appear to them to be suitable to their nature and profitable! And yet in a manner you do not allow them to do this, when you are vexed because they do wrong. For they are certainly moved towards things because they suppose them to be suitable to their nature and profitable to them. – But it is not so. – Teach them then, and show them without being angry.

28.   Death is a cessation of the impressions through the senses, and of the pulling of the strings which move the

appetites, and of the discursive movements of the thoughts, and of the service to the flesh.

29.   It is a shame for the soul to be first to give way in this life, when your body does not give way.

30.   Take care that you are not made into a Caesar, that you are not dyed with this dye, for such things happen. Keep yourself then simple, good, pure, serious, free from affectation, a friend of justice, a worshipper of the gods, kind, affectionate, strenuous in all proper acts. Strive to continue to be such as philosophy wished to make you. Revere the gods, and help men. Life is short. There is only one fruit of this terrene life – a pious disposition and social acts. Do everything as a disciple of Antoninus. Remember his constancy in every act which was conformable to reason, and his evenness in all things, and his piety, and the serenity of his countenance, and his sweetness, and his disregard of empty fame, and his efforts to understand things. And how he would never let anything pass without having first most carefully examined it and clearly understood it. And how he bore with those who blamed him unjustly without blaming them in return. How he did nothing in a hurry, and how he listened not to calumnies, and how exact an examiner of manners and actions he was, and not given to reproach people, nor timid, nor suspicious, nor a sophist. And with how little he was satisfied, such as lodging, bed, dress, food, servants. And how laborious and patient, and how he was able on account of his sparing diet to hold out to the evening, not even requiring to relieve himself by any evacuations except at the usual hour. And his firmness and uniformity in his friendships, and how he tolerated freedom of speech in those who opposed his opinions, and the pleasure

that he had when any man showed him anything better. And how religious he was without superstition. Imitate all this, that you may have as good a conscience, when your last hour comes, as he had.

31.   Return to your sober senses and call yourself back. And when you hast roused yourself from sleep and have perceived that they were only dreams which troubled you, now in your waking hours look at these [the things about you] as you did look at those [dreams].

32.   I consist of a little body and a soul. Now to this little body all things are indifferent, for it is not able to perceive differences. But to the understanding those things only are indifferent which are not the works of its own activity. But whatever things are the works of its own activity, all these are in its power. And of these however only those which are done with reference to the present. For as to the future and the past activities of the mind, even these are for the present indifferent.

33.   Neither the labour which the hand does nor that of the foot is contrary to nature, so long as the foot does the foot's work and the hand the hand's. So then neither to a man as a man is his labour contrary to nature, so long as it does the things of a man. But if the labour is not contrary to his nature, neither is it an evil to him.

34.   How many pleasures have been enjoyed by robbers, patricides, tyrants.

35.   Do you not see how the handicrafts-men accommodate themselves up to a certain point to those who are not skilled in their craft – nevertheless they cling to the reason [the principles] of their art, and do not endure to depart from it? Is it not strange if the architect and the physician shall have

more respect to the reason [the principles] of their own arts than man to his own reason, which is common to him and the gods?

36.   Asia, Europe, are corners of the universe; all the sea a drop in the universe; Athos a little clod of the universe: all the present time is a point in eternity. All things are little, changeable, perishable. All things come from thence, from that universal ruling power, either directly proceeding or by way of sequence. And accordingly the lion's gaping jaws, and that which is poisonous, and every harmful thing, as a thorn, as mud, are after-products of the grand and beautiful. Do not then imagine that they are of another kind from that which you venerate, but form a just opinion of the source of all.

37.   He who has seen present things has seen all, both everything which has taken place from all eternity and everything which will be for time without end, for all things are of one kin and of one form.

38.   Frequently consider the connection of all things in the universe and their relation to one another. For in a manner all things are implicated with one another, and all in this way are friendly to one another. For one thing comes in order after another, and this is by virtue of the active movement and mutual conspiration and the unity of the substance.

39.   Adapt yourself to the things with which your lot has been cast: and the men among whom you have received your portion, love them, but do it truly.

40.   Every instrument, tool, vessel, if it does that for which it has been made, is well, and yet he who made it is not there. But in the things which are held together by nature there is

within, and there abides in them the power which made them; wherefore the more is it fit to revere this power, and to think, that, if you do live and act according to its will, everything in you is in conformity to intelligence. And thus also in the universe the things which belong to it are in conformity to intelligence.

41.   Whatever of the things which are not within your power you shall suppose to be good for you or evil, it must necessarily be that, if such a bad thing befall you, or the loss of such a good thing, you will not blame the gods, and hate men too, those who are the cause of the misfortune or the loss, or those who are suspected of being likely to be the cause. And indeed we do much injustice because we make a difference between these things [i.e., because we do not regard these things as indifferent]. But if we judge only those things which are in our power to be good or bad, there remains no reason either for finding fault with God or standing in a hostile attitude to man.

42.   We are all working together to one end, some with knowledge and design, and others without knowing what they do. As men also when they are asleep, of whom it is Heraclitus, I think, who says that they are labourers and co-operators in the things which take place in the universe. But men co-operate after different fashions, and even those co-operate abundantly, who find fault with what happens and those who try to oppose it and to hinder it. For the universe had need even of such men as these. It remains then for you to understand among what kind of workmen you place yourself. For he who rules all things will certainly make a right use of you, and he will receive you among some part of the co-operators and of those whose labours conduce to one end. But do not be such a part as

the mean and ridiculous verse in the play, of which Chrysippus speaks.

43.　Does the sun undertake to do the work of the rain, or Asclepius the work of the Fruit-bearer [the earth]? And how is it with respect to each of the stars – are they not different and yet they work together to the same end?

44.　If the gods have determined about me and about the things which must happen to me, they have determined well, for it is not easy even to imagine a deity without forethought. And as to doing me harm, why should they have any desire towards that? For what advantage would result to them from this or to the whole, which is the special object of their providence? But if they have not determined about me individually, they have certainly determined about the whole at least, and the things which happen by way of sequence in this general arrangement I ought to accept with pleasure and to be content with them. But if they determine about nothing – which it is wicked to believe, or if we do believe it, let us neither sacrifice nor pray nor swear by them, nor do anything else which we do as if the gods were present and lived with us – but if however the gods determine about none of the things which concern us, I am able to determine about myself, and I can inquire about that which is useful. And that is useful to every man which is conformable to his own constitution and nature. But my nature is rational and social, and my city and country, so far as I am Antoninus, is Rome, but so far as I am a man, it is the world. The things then which are useful to these cities are alone useful to me.

45.　Whatever happens to every man, this is for the interest of the universal: this might be sufficient. But further you will observe this also as a general truth, if you observe, that whatever is profitable to any man is profitable also to other men. But let the word profitable be taken here in the common sense as said of things of the middle kind [neither good nor bad].

46. As it happens to you in the amphitheatre and such places, that the continual sight of the same things, and the uniformity, make the spectacle wearisome, so it is in the whole of life; for all things above, below, are the same and from the same. How long then?

47. Think continually that all kinds of men and all kinds of pursuits and of all nations are dead, so that your thoughts come down even to Philistion and Phoebus and Origanion. Now turn your thoughts to the other kinds [of men]. To that place then we must remove, where there are so many great orators, and so many noble philosophers, Heraclitus, Pythagoras, Socrates. So many heroes of former days, and so many generals after them, and tyrants. Besides these, Eudoxus, Hipparchus, Archimedes, and other men of acute natural talents, great minds, lovers of labour, versatile, confident, mockers even of the perishable and ephemeral life of man, as Menippus and such as are like him. As to all these consider that they have long been in the dust. What harm then is this to them; and what to those whose names are altogether unknown? One thing here is worth a great deal, to pass your life in truth and justice, with a benevolent disposition even to liars and unjust men.

48. When you wish to delight yourself, think of the virtues of those who live with you. For instance, the activity of one, and the modesty of another, and the liberality of a third, and some other good quality of a fourth. For nothing delights so

much as the examples of the virtues, when they are exhibited in the morals of those who live with us and present themselves in abundance, as far as is possible. Hence we must keep them before us.

49. You are not dissatisfied. I suppose, because you weigh only so many litrae and not three hundred. Be not dissatisfied then that you must live only so many years and not more. For as you are satisfied with the amount of substance which has been assigned to you, so be content with the time.

50. Let us try to persuade them [men]. But act even against their will, when the principles of justice lead that way. If however any man by using force stands in your way, bring yourself to contentment and tranquillity, and at the same time employ the hindrance towards the exercise of some other virtue. And remember that your attempt was with a reservation [conditionally], that you did not desire to do impossibilities. What then did you desire? – Some such effort as this. – But you attain your object if the things to which you were moved are [not] accomplished.

51. He who loves fame considers another man's activity to be his own good, and he who loves pleasure, his own sensations. But he who has understanding considers his own acts to be his own good.

52. It is in our power to have no opinion about a thing, and not to be disturbed in our soul. For things themselves have no natural power to form our judgments.

53. Accustom yourself to attend carefully to what is said by another, and as much as it is possible, be in the speaker's mind.

54.   That which is not good for the swarm, neither is it good for the bee.

55.   If sailors abused the helmsman, or the sick the doctor, would they listen to anybody else? Or how could the helmsman secure the safety of those in the ship, or the doctor the health of those whom he attends?

56.   How many together with whom I came into the world are already gone out of it.

57.   To the jaundiced honey tastes bitter, and to those bitten by mad dogs water causes fear, and to little children the ball is a fine thing. Why then am I angry? Do you think that a false opinion has less power than the bile in the jaundiced or the poison in him who is bitten by a mad dog?

58.   No man will hinder you from living according to the reason of your own nature: nothing will happen to you contrary to the reason of the universal nature.

59.   What kind of people are those whom men wish to please, and for what objects, and by what kind of acts? How soon will time cover all things, and how many it has covered already.

BOOK SEVEN

1. What is badness? It is that which you have often seen. And on the occasion of everything which happens keep this in mind, that it is that which you have often seen. Everywhere up and down you will find the same things, with which the old histories are filled, those of the middle ages and those of our own day, with which cities and houses are filled now. There is nothing new: all things are both familiar and short-lived.

2. How can our principles become dead, unless the impressions [thoughts] which correspond to them are extinguished? But it is in your power continuously to fan these thoughts into a flame. I can have that opinion about anything which I ought to have. If I can, why am I disturbed? The things which are external to my mind have no relation at all to my mind. – Let this be the state of your affects, and you stand erect. To recover your life is in your power. Look at things again as you used to look at them for in this consists the recovery of your life.

3. The idle business of show, plays on the stage, flocks of sheep, herds, exercises with spears, a bone cast to little dogs, a bit of bread into fishponds, labourings of ants and burden-carrying, runnings about of frightened little mice, puppets pulled by strings – [all alike]. It is your duty then in the midst of such things to show good humour and not a proud air, to

understand however that every man is worth just so much as the things are worth about which he busies himself.

4. In discourse you must attend to what is said, and in every movement you must observe what is being done. And in the one you should see immediately to what end it refers, but in the other watch carefully what is the thing signified.

5. Is my understanding sufficient for this or not? If it is sufficient, I use it for the work as an instrument given by the universal nature. But if it is not sufficient, then either I retire from the work and give way to him who is able to do it better, unless there is some reason why I ought not to do so or I do it as well as I can, taking to help me the man who with the aid of my ruling principle can do what is now fit and useful for the general good. For whatsoever I can do either by myself or with another, ought to be directed to this only, to that which is useful and well suited to society.

6. How many after being celebrated by fame have been given up to oblivion, and how many who have celebrated the fame of others have long been dead.

7. Be not ashamed to be helped for it is your business to do your duty like a soldier in the assault on a town. How then, if being lame you cannot mount up on the battlements alone, but with the help of another it is possible?

8. Let not future things disturb you, for you will come to them, if it shall be necessary, having with you the same reason which you now use for present things.

9. All things are implicated with one another, and the bond is holy, and there is hardly anything unconnected with any other thing. For things have been coordinated, and they

combine to form the same universe. For there is one universe made up of all things, and one god who pervades all things, and one substance, and one law, [one] common reason in all intelligent animals, and one truth; if indeed there is also one perfection for all animals which are of the same stock and participate in the reason.

10. Everything material soon disappears in the substance of the whole, and everything formal [causal] is very soon taken back into the universal reason, and the memory of everything is very soon overwhelmed in time.

11. To the rational animal the same act is according to nature and according to reason.

12. Be erect, or be made erect.

13. Just as it is with the members in those bodies which are united in one, so it is with rational beings which exist separate, for they have been constituted for one cooperation. And the perception of this will be more apparent to you if you often say to yourself that I am a member [μέλος] of the system of rational beings. But if [substituting the letter ρ for λ] you say that you are a part [μέρος], you do not yet love men from your heart, beneficence does not yet delight you for its own sake, you still do it barely as a thing of propriety, and not yet as doing good to yourself.

14. Let there fall externally what will on the parts which can feel the effects of this fall. For those parts which have felt will complain, if they choose. But I, unless I think that what has happened is an evil, am not injured. And it is in my power not to think so.

15. Whatever anyone does or says, I must be good; just as if the gold, or the emerald, or the purple, were always

saying this. Whatever anyone does or says, I must be emerald and keep my colour.

16.   The ruling faculty does not disturb itself. I mean, does not frighten itself or cause itself pain. But if anyone else can frighten or pain it, let him do so. For the faculty itself will not by its own opinion turn itself into such ways. Let the body itself take care, if it can, that it suffer nothing, and let it speak, if it suffers. But the soul itself, that which is subject to fear, to pain, which has completely the power of forming an opinion about these things, will suffer nothing, for it will never deviate into such a judgment. The leading principle in itself wants nothing, unless it makes a want for itself. Therefore it is both free from perturbation and unimpeded, if it does not disturb and impede itself.

17.   Happiness [eudaemonia] is a good daemon, or a good thing. What then are you doing here, O imagination? Go away, I entreat you by the gods, as you did come, for I do not want you. But you have come according to your old fashion. I am not angry with you: just go away.

18.   Is any man afraid of change? Why, what can take place without change? What then is more pleasing or more suitable to the universal nature? And can you take a bath unless the wood undergoes a change? Can you be nourished, unless the food undergoes a change? And can anything else that is useful be accomplished without change? Do you not see then that for yourself also to change is just the same, and equally necessary for the universal nature?

19.   Through the universal substance as through a furious torrent all bodies are carried, being by their nature united with and cooperating with the whole, as the parts of our body with

one another. How many a Chrysippus, how many a Socrates, how many an Epictetus has time already swallowed up! And let the same thought occur to you with reference to every man and thing.

20.   One thing only troubles me, lest I should do something which the constitution of man does not allow, or in the way which it does not allow, or what it does not allow now.

21.   Near is your forgetfulness of all things, and near the forgetfulness of you by all.

22.   It is peculiar to man to love even those who do wrong. And this happens, if when they do wrong it occurs to you that they are kinsmen, and that they do wrong through ignorance and unintentionally, and that soon both of you will die; and above all, that the wrongdoer has done you no harm, for he has not made your ruling faculty worse than it was before.

23.   The universal nature out of the universal substance, as if it were wax, now moulds a horse, and when it has broken this up, it uses the material for a tree, then for a man, then for something else; and each of these things subsists for a very short time. But it is no hardship for the vessel to be broken up, just as there was none in its being fastened together.

24.   A scowling look is altogether unnatural. When it is often assumed, the result is that all comeliness dies away, and at last is so completely extinguished that it cannot be again lighted up at all. Try to conclude from this very fact that it is contrary to reason. For if even the perception of doing wrong shall depart, what reason is there for living any longer?

25.   Nature which governs the whole will soon change all things you see, and out of their substance will make other

things, and again other things from the substance of them, in order that the world may be ever new.

26.   When a man has done you any wrong, immediately consider with what opinion about good or evil he has done wrong. For when you have seen this, you will pity him, and will neither wonder nor be angry. For either you yourself think the same thing to be good that he does, or another thing of the same kind. It is your duty then to pardon him. But if you do not think such things to be good or evil, you will more readily be well disposed to him who is in error.

27.   Think not so much of what you have not as of what you have. Select the best of the things which you have and then reflect how eagerly they would have been sought if you had them not. At the same time, however, take care that you do not through being so pleased with them accustom yourself to overvalue them, so as to be disturbed if ever you should not have them.

28.   Retire into yourself. The rational principle which rules has this nature, that it is content with itself when it does what is just, and so secures tranquillity.

29.   Wipe out the imagination. Stop the pulling of the strings. Confine yourself to the present. Understand well what happens either to you or to another. Divide and distribute every object into the causal and the material. Think of your last hour. Let the wrong which is done by a man stay there where the wrong was done.

30.   Direct your attention to what is said. Let your understanding enter into the things that are doing and the things which do them.

31.   Adorn yourself with simplicity and modesty, and with indifference towards the things which lie between virtue and vice. Love mankind. Follow God. The poet says that law rules all – And it is enough to remember that law rules all.

32.   About death: whether it is a dispersion, or a resolution into atoms, or annihilation, it is either extinction or change.

33.   About pain: the pain which is intolerable carries us off but that which lasts a long time is tolerable. The mind maintains its own tranquillity by retiring into itself, and the ruling faculty is not made worse. But the parts which are harmed by pain, let them, if they can, give their opinion about it.

34.   About fame: look at the minds [of those who seek fame], observe what they are, and what kind of things they avoid, and what kind of things they pursue. And consider that as the heaps of sand piled on one another hide the former sands; so in life the events which go before are soon covered by those which come after.

35.   From Plato: The man who has an elevated mind and takes a view of all time and of all substance, do you suppose it possible for him to think that human life is anything great? It is not possible, he said. – Such a man then will think that death also is no evil. – Certainly not.

36.   From Antisthenes: It is royal to do good and to be abused.

37.   It is a base thing for the countenance to be obedient and to regulate and compose itself as the mind commands, and for the mind not to be regulated and composed by itself.

38.   It is not right to vex ourselves at things, for they care nought about it.

39.   To the immortal gods and us give joy.

40.   Life must be reaped like the ripe ears of corn. One man is born; another dies.

41.   If gods care not for me and my children, there is a reason for it.

42.   For the good is with me, and the just.

43.   No joining others in their wailing, no violent emotion.

44.   From Plato: But I would make this man a sufficient answer, which is this: you say not well, if you think that a man who is good for anything at all ought to weigh the hazard of life or death, and should not rather look to this only in all that he does: whether he is doing what is just or unjust, and the works of a good or bad man.

45.   For thus it is, men of Athens, in truth: wherever a man has placed himself thinking it the best place for him, or has been placed by a commander, there in my opinion he ought to stay and to abide the hazard, taking nothing into the reckoning, either death or anything else, before the baseness [of deserting his post].

46.   But, my good friend, reflect whether that which is noble and good is not something different from saving and being saved. For as to a man living such or such a time, at least one who is really a man, consider if this is not a thing to be dismissed from the thoughts. And there must be no love of life but as to these matters a man must intrust them to the Deity and believe what the women say, that no man can escape his

destiny, the next inquiry being how he may best live the time that he has to live.

47.   Look round at the courses of the stars, as if you were going along with them, and constantly consider the changes of the elements into one another, for such thoughts purge away the filth of earthly life.

48.   This is a fine saying of Plato: That he who is discoursing about men should look also at earthly things as if he viewed them from some higher place. He should look at them in their assemblies, armies, agricultural labours, marriages, treaties, births, deaths, noise of the courts of justice, desert places, various nations of barbarians, feasts, lamentations, markets, a mixture of all things and an orderly combination of contraries.

49.   Consider the past – such great changes of political supremacies. You may foresee also the things which will be. For they will certainly be of like form, and it is not possible that they should deviate from the order of the things which take place now. Accordingly to have contemplated human life for forty years is the same as to have contemplated it for ten thousand years. For what more will you see?

50.   That which has grown from the earth to the earth,

But that which has sprung from heavenly seed,

Back to the heavenly realms returns.

This is either a dissolution of the mutual involution of the atoms, or a similar dispersion of the insentient elements.

51.   With food and drinks and cunning magic arts

Turning the channel's course to 'scape from death.

The breeze which heaven has sent

We must endure, and toil without complaining.

52.   Another may be more expert in casting his opponent but he is not more social, nor more modest, nor better disciplined to meet all that happens, nor more considerate with respect to the faults of his neighbours.

53.   Where any work can be done conformably to the reason which is common to gods and men, there we have nothing to fear. For where we are able to get profit by means of the activity which is successful and proceeds according to our constitution, there no harm is to be suspected.

54.   Everywhere and at all times it is in your power piously to acquiesce in your present condition, and to behave justly to those who are about you, and to exert your skill upon your present thoughts, that nothing shall steal into them without being well examined.

55.   Do not look around you to discover other men's ruling principles, but look straight to this, to what nature leads you, both the universal nature through the things which happen to you, and your own nature through the acts which must be done by you. But every being ought to do that which is according to its constitution. And all other things have been constituted for the sake of rational beings, just as among irrational things the inferior for the sake of the superior, but the rational for the sake of one another.

The prime principle then in man's constitution is the social. And the second is not to yield to the persuasions of the body – for it is the peculiar office of the rational and intelligent motion to circumscribe itself, and never to be overpowered either by the motion of the senses or of the appetites. For both are animal: but the intelligent motion claims superiority, and does not permit itself to be overpowered by the others.

And with good reason, for it is formed by nature to use all of them. The third thing in the rational constitution is freedom from error and from deception. Then let the ruling principle holding fast to these things go straight on, and it has what is its own.

56.   Consider yourself to be dead, and to have completed your life up to the present time, and live according to nature the remainder which is allowed you.

57.   Love only that which happens to you and is spun with the thread of your destiny. For what is more suitable?

58.   In everything which happens keep before your eyes those to whom the same things happened, and how they were vexed, and treated them as strange things, and found fault with them: and now where are they? Nowhere. Why then do you too choose to act in the same way? And why do you not leave these agitations which are foreign to nature to those who cause them and those who are moved by them. And why are you not altogether intent upon the right way of making use of the things which happen to you? For then you will use them well, and they will be a material for you [to work on]. Only attend to yourself, and resolve to be a good man in every act which you do: and remember...

59.   Look within. Within is the fountain of good, and it will ever bubble up, if you will ever dig.

60.   The body ought to be compact, and to show no irregularity either in motion or attitude. For what the mind shows in the face by maintaining in it the expression of intelligence and propriety, that ought to be required also in the whole body. But all these things should be observed without affectation.

61.   The art of life is more like the wrestler's art than the dancer's, in respect of this, that it should stand ready and firm to meet onsets which are sudden and unexpected.

62.   Constantly observe who those are whose approbation you wish to have, and what ruling principles they possess. For then you will neither blame those who offend involuntarily, nor will you want their approbation, if you look to the sources of their opinions and appetites.

63.   Every soul, the philosopher says, is involuntarily deprived of truth. Consequently in the same way it is deprived of justice and temperance and benevolence and everything of the kind. It is most necessary to bear this constantly in mind, for thus you will be more gentle towards all.

64.   In every pain let this thought be present, that there is no dishonour in it, nor does it make the governing intelligence worse, for it does not damage the intelligence either so far as the intelligence is rational or so far as it is social. Indeed in the case of most pains let this remark of Epicurus aid you, that pain is neither intolerable nor everlasting, if you bear in mind that it has its limits, and if you add nothing to it in imagination. And remember this too, that we do not perceive that many things which are disagreeable to us are the same as pain, such as excessive drowsiness, and the being scorched by heat, and the having no appetite. When then you are discontented about any of these things, say to yourself that you are yielding to pain.

65.   Take care not to feel towards the inhuman as they feel towards men.

66.   How do we know if Telauges was not superior in character to Socrates? For it is not enough that Socrates

died a more noble death, and disputed more skilfully with the sophists, and passed the night in the cold with more endurance, and that when he was bid to arrest Leon of Salamis, he considered it more noble to refuse, and that he walked in a swaggering way in the streets – though as to this fact one may have great doubts if it was true. But we ought to inquire what kind of a soul it was that Socrates possessed, and if he was able to be content with being just towards men and pious towards the gods, neither idly vexed on account of men's villainy, nor yet making himself a slave to any man's ignorance, nor receiving as strange anything that fell to his share out of the universal, nor enduring it as intolerable, nor allowing his understanding to sympathize with the affects of the miserable flesh.

67.   Nature has not so mingled [the intelligence] with the composition of the body, as not to have allowed you the power of circumscribing yourself and of bringing under subjection to yourself all that is your own. For it is very possible to be a divine man and to be recognized as such by no one. Always bear this in mind; and another thing too, that very little indeed is necessary for living a happy life. And because you hast despaired of becoming a dialectician and skilled in the knowledge of nature, do not for this reason renounce the hope of being both free and modest, and social and obedient to God.

68.   It is in your power to live free from all compulsion in the greatest tranquillity of mind, even if all the world cry out against you as much as they choose, and even if wild beasts tear in pieces the members of this kneaded matter which has grown around you. For what hinders the mind in the midst of all this from maintaining itself in tranquillity and in a just

judgment of all surrounding things and in a ready use of the objects which are presented to it, so that the judgment may say to the thing which falls under its observation: This you are in substance [reality], though in men's opinion you may appear to be of a different kind. And the use shall say to that which falls under the hand: you are the thing that I was seeking. For to me that which presents itself is always a material for virtue both rational and political, and in a word, for the exercise of art, which belongs to man or God. For everything which happens has a relationship either to God or man, and is neither new nor difficult to handle, but usual and apt matter to work on.

69.   The perfection of moral character consists in this, in passing every day as the last, and in being neither violently excited nor torpid nor playing the hypocrite.

70.   The gods who are immortal are not vexed because during so long a time they must tolerate continually men such as they are and so many of them bad. And besides this, they also take care of them in all ways. But you, who are destined to end so soon, are you wearied of enduring the bad, and this too when you are one of them?

71.   It is a ridiculous thing for a man not to fly from his own badness, which is indeed possible, but to fly from other men's badness, which is impossible.

72.   Whatever the rational and political [social] faculty finds to be neither intelligent nor social, it properly judges to be inferior to itself.

73.   When you have done a good act and another has received it, why do you still look for a third thing besides these, as fools do, either to have the reputation of having done a good act or to obtain a return?

74.   No man is tired of receiving what is useful. But it is useful to act according to nature. Do not then be tired of receiving what is useful by doing it to others.

75.   The nature of the All moved to make the universe. But now either everything that takes place comes by way of consequence or [continuity], or even the chief things towards which the ruling power of the universe directs its own movement are governed by no rational principle. If this is remembered, it will make you more tranquil in many things.

BOOK EIGHT

1.   This reflection also tends to the removal of the desire of empty fame, that it is no longer in your power to have lived the whole of your life, or at least your life from your youth upwards, like a philosopher, but both to many others and to yourself it is plain that you are far from philosophy. You have fallen into disorder then, so that it is no longer easy for you to get the reputation of a philosopher and your plan of life also opposes it. If then you have truly seen where the matter lies, throw away the thought of how you shall seem [to others], and be content if you shall live the rest of your life in such ways as your nature wills. Observe then what it wills, and let nothing else distract you. For you have had experience of many wanderings without having found happiness anywhere – not in syllogisms, nor in wealth, nor in reputation, nor in enjoyment, nor anywhere. Where is it then? In doing what man's nature requires. How then shall a man do this? If he has principles from which come his affects and his acts. What principles? Those which relate to good and bad: the belief that there is nothing good for man which does not make him just, temperate, manly, free, and that there is nothing bad which does not do the contrary to what has been mentioned.

2.   On the occasion of every act ask yourself, "How is this with respect to me? Shall I repent of it?" A little time and I am dead, and all is gone. What more do I seek, if what I am now

doing is the work of an intelligent living being, and a social being, and one who is under the same law with God?

3. Alexander the Great and Julius Caesar and Pompey the Great, what are they in comparison with Diogenes [the Cynic] and Heraclitus and Socrates? For they were acquainted with things, and their causes [forms], and their matter, and the ruling principles of these men were the same [or conformable to their pursuits]. But as to the others, how many things had they for which to care, and to how many things were they slaves!

4. [Consider] that men will do the same things nevertheless, even though you should burst.

5. This is the chief thing: Do not be perturbed, for all things are according to the nature of the universal, and in a little time you will be nobody and nowhere, like Hadrian and Augustus. In the next place, having fixed your eyes steadily on your business, look at it, and at the same time remembering that it is your duty to be a good man, and what man's nature demands, do that without turning aside; and speak as it seems to you most just, only let it be with a good disposition and with modesty and without hypocrisy.

6. The nature of the universal has this work to do – to remove to that place the things which are in this, to change them, to take them away hence, and to carry them there. All things are change, yet we need not fear anything new. All things are familiar [to us] but the distribution of them still remains the same.

7. Every nature is contented with itself when it goes on its way well and a rational nature goes on its way well when in its thoughts it assents to nothing false or uncertain, and

when it directs its movements to social acts only, and when it confines its desires and aversions to the things which are in its power, and when it is satisfied with everything that is assigned to it by the common nature. For of this common nature every particular nature is a part, as the nature of the leaf is a part of the nature of the plant, except that in the plant the nature of the leaf is part of a nature which has not perception or reason, and is subject to be impeded. But the nature of man is part of a nature which is not subject to impediments, and is intelligent and just, since it gives to everything in equal portions and according to its worth, times, substance, cause [form], activity, and incident. But examine, not to discover that any one thing compared with any other single thing is equal in all respects, but by taking all the parts together of one thing and comparing them with all the parts together of another.

8.   You do not have leisure [or ability] to read. But you have leisure [or ability] to check arrogance, leisure to be superior to pleasure and pain, leisure to be superior to love of fame, and not to be vexed at stupid and ungrateful people, nor even to care for them.

9.   Let no man any longer hear you finding fault with the court life or with your own.

10.   Repentance is a kind of self-reproof for having neglected something useful. But that which is good must be something useful, and the perfect good man should look after it. But no such man would ever repent of having refused any sensual pleasure. Pleasure then is neither good nor useful.

11.   This thing, what is it in itself, in its own constitution? What is its substance and material? And what its causal nature

[or form]? And what is it doing in the world? And how long does it subsist?

12.   When you rise from sleep with reluctance, remember that it is according to your constitution and according to human nature to perform social acts, but sleeping is common also to irrational animals. But that which is according to each individual's nature is also more peculiarly its own, and more suitable to its nature, and indeed also more agreeable.

13.   Constantly, and, if it is possible, on the occasion of every impression on the soul, apply to it the principles of Physics, Ethics, and Dialectic.

14.   Whatever man you meet with, immediately say to yourself: "What opinions has this man about good and bad?" For if with respect to pleasure and pain and the causes of each, and with respect to fame and ignominy, death and life, he has such and such opinions, it will seem nothing wonderful or strange to me if he does such and such things, and I shall bear in mind that he is compelled to do so.

15.   Remember that as it is shameful to be surprised if the fig-tree produces figs, so it is to be surprised if the world produces such and such things of which it is productive. And for the physician and the helmsman it is shameful to be surprised if a man has a fever, or if the wind is unfavourable.

16.   Remember that to change your opinion and to follow him who corrects your error is as consistent with freedom as it is to persist in your error. For it is your own, the activity which is exerted according to your own movement and judgment, and indeed according to your own understanding too.

17. If a thing is in your own power, why do you do it? But if it is in the power of another, whom do you blame – the atoms [chance] or the gods? Both are foolish; you must blame nobody. For if you can, correct [that which is the cause]; but if you cannot do this, correct at least the thing itself. But if you cannot do even this, of what use is it to you to find fault? For nothing should be done without a purpose.

18. That which has died does not fall out of the universe. If it stays here, it also changes here, and is dissolved into its proper parts, which are elements of the universe and of yourself. And these too change, and they murmur not.

19. Everything exists for some end – a horse, a vine. Why do you wonder? Even the sun will say, "I am for some purpose", and the rest of the gods will say the same. For what purpose then are you – to enjoy pleasure? See if common sense allows this.

20. Nature has had regard in everything no less to the end than to the beginning and the continuance, just like the man who throws up a ball. What good is it then for the ball to be thrown up, or harm for it to come down, or even to have fallen? and what good is it to the bubble while it holds together, or what harm when it is burst? The same may be said of a light also.

21. Turn it [the body] inside out, and see what kind of thing it is, and when it has grown old, what kind of thing it becomes, and when it is diseased.

Short lived are both the praiser and the praised, and the rememberer and the remembered. And all this in a nook of this part of the world, and not even here do all agree, no, not anyone with himself. And the whole earth too is but a small point.

22.   Attend to the matter which is before you, whether it is an opinion or an act or a word.

You suffer this justly: for you choose rather to become good tomorrow than to be good today.

23.   Am I doing anything? I do it with reference to the good of mankind. Does anything happen to me? I receive it and refer it to the gods, and the source of all things, from which all that happens is derived.

24.   Such as bathing appears to you – oil, sweat, dirt, filthy water, all things disgusting – so is every part of life and everything.

25.   Lucilla [my mother] saw Verus [my father] die, and then Lucilla died. Secunda saw Maximus die, and then Secunda died. Epitynchanus saw Diotimus die, and then Epitynchanus died. Antoninus saw [his wife] Faustina die, and then Antoninus died. Such is everything. Celer saw Hadrian die, and then Celer died. And those sharp-witted men, either seers or men inflated with pride, where are they – for instance the sharp-witted men, Charax and Demetrius the Platonist, and Eudaemon, and anyone else like them? All ephemeral, dead long ago. Some indeed have not been remembered even for a short time, and others have become the heroes of fables, and again others have disappeared even from fables. Remember this then, that this little compound, yourself, must either be dissolved, or your poor breath must be extinguished, or be removed and placed elsewhere.

26.   It is satisfaction for a man to do the proper works of a man. Now it is a proper work of a man to be benevolent to

his own kind, to despise the movements of the senses, to form a just judgment of plausible appearances, and to take a survey of the nature of the universe and of the things which happen in it.

27. There are three relations [between you and other things]: the one to the body which surrounds you, the second to the divine cause from which all things come to all, and the third to those who live with you.

28. Pain is either an evil to the body – then let the body say what it thinks of it – or to the soul. But it is in the power of the soul to maintain its own serenity and tranquillity, and not to think that pain is an evil. For every judgment and movement and desire and aversion is within, and no evil ascends so high.

29. Wipe out your imaginations by often saying to yourself: "Now it is in my power to let no badness be in this soul, nor desire, nor any perturbation at all but looking at all things I see what is their nature, and I use each according to its value." – Remember this power which you have from nature.

30. Speak both in the senate and to every man, whoever he may be, appropriately, not with any affectation: use plain discourse.

31. Augustus' court, wife, daughter, descendants, ancestors, sister, Agrippa, kinsmen, intimates, friends; Areius, Maecenas, physicians, and sacrificing priests – the whole court is dead. Then turn to the rest, not considering the death of a single man [but of a whole race], as of the Pompeii; and that which is inscribed on the tombs: "The last of his race." Then consider what trouble those before them have had that they might leave a successor, and then that of necessity some one

must be the last. Again, here consider the death of a whole race.

32.　It is your duty to order your life well in every single act, and if every act does its duty as far as is possible, be content, and no one is able to hinder you so that each act shall not do its duty. – But something external will stand in the way. – Nothing will stand in the way of your acting justly and soberly and considerately. – But perhaps some other active power will be hindered. – Well, but by acquiescing in the hindrance and by being content to transfer your efforts to that which is allowed, another opportunity of action is immediately put before you in place of that which was hindered, and one which will adapt itself to this ordering of which we are speaking.

33.　Receive [wealth or prosperity] without arrogance, and be ready to let it go.

34.　If you ever saw a hand cut off, or a foot, or a head, lying anywhere apart from the rest of the body, such does a man make himself, as far as he can, who is not content with what happens, and separates himself from others, or does anything unsocial. Suppose that you have detached yourself from the natural unity – for you were made by nature a part, but now you have cut yourself off – yet here there is this beautiful provision, that it is in your power again to unite yourself. God has allowed this to no other part, after it has been separated and cut asunder, to come together again. But consider the kindness by which he has distinguished man, for he has put it in his power not to be separated at all from the universal. And when he has been separated, he has allowed him to return and to be united and to resume his place as a part.

35.   As the nature of the universal has given to every rational being all the other powers that it has, so we have received from it this power also. For as the universal nature converts and fixes in its predestined place everything which stands in the way and opposes it, and makes such things a part of itself, so also the rational animal is able to make every hindrance its own material, and to use it for such purposes as it may have designed.

36.   Do not disturb yourself by thinking of the whole of your life. Do not let your thoughts at once embrace all the various troubles which you may expect to befall you. But on every occasion ask yourself, "What is there in this which is intolerable and past bearing?" For you will be ashamed to confess it. In the next place remember that neither the future nor the past pains you, but only the present. But this is reduced to a very little, if you only circumscribe it, and chide your mind if it is unable to hold out against even this.

37.   Does Panthea or Fergamus now sit by the tomb of [Lucius] Verus? Does Chaurias or Diotimus sit by the tomb of Hadrian? That would be ridiculous. Well, suppose they did sit there, would the dead be conscious of it? And if the dead were conscious, would they be pleased? And if they were pleased, would that make them immortal? Was it not in the order of destiny that these persons too should first become old women and old men and then die? What then would those do after these were dead? All this is foul smell and blood in a bag.

38.   If you can see sharp, look and judge wisely, says the philosopher.

39. In the constitution of the rational animal I see no virtue which is opposed to justice but I see a virtue which is opposed to love of pleasure, and that is temperance.

40. If you take away your opinion about that which appears to give you pain, you yourself stand in perfect security. – Who is this self? – The reason. – But I am not reason. – Be it so. Let then the reason itself not trouble itself. But if any other part of you suffers, let it have its own opinion about itself.

41. Hindrance to the perceptions of sense is an evil to the animal nature. Hindrance to the movements [desires] is equally an evil to the animal nature. And something else also is equally an impediment and an evil to the constitution of plants. So then that which is a hindrance to the intelligence is an evil to the intelligent nature. Apply all these things then to yourself. Does pain or sensuous pleasure affect you? The senses will look to that. Has any obstacle opposed you in your efforts towards an object? If indeed you were making this effort absolutely [unconditionally, or without any reservation], certainly this obstacle is an evil to you considered as a rational animal. But if you take [into consideration] the usual course of things, you have not yet been injured nor even impeded. The things however which are proper to the understanding no other man is used to impede, for neither fire, nor iron, nor tyrant, nor abuse, touches it in any way. When it has been made a sphere, it continues a sphere.

42. It is not fit that I should give myself pain, for I have never intentionally given pain even to another.

43. Different things delight different people but it is my delight to keep the ruling faculty sound without turning away

either from any man or from any of the things which happen to men, but looking at and receiving all with welcome eyes and using everything according to its value.

44.   See that you secure this present time to yourself for those who rather pursue posthumous fame do not consider that men in the future will be exactly like these whom they cannot bear now, and both are mortal. And what is it anyway to you if these men of after time utter this or that sound, or have this or that opinion about you?

45.   Take me and cast me where you will. For there I shall keep my divine part tranquil, that is, content, if it can feel and act comformably to its proper constitution. Is this [change of place] sufficient reason why my soul should be unhappy and worse than it was, depressed, expanded, shrinking, affrighted? And what will you find which is sufficient reason for this?

46.   Nothing can happen to any man which is not a human accident, nor to an ox which is not according to the nature of an ox, nor to a vine which is not according to the nature of a vine, nor to a stone which is not proper to a stone. If then there happens to each thing both what is usual and natural, why should you complain? For the common nature brings nothing which may not be borne by you.

47.   If you are pained by any external thing, it is not this thing that disturbs you, but your own judgment about it. And it is in your power to wipe out this judgment now. But if anything in your own disposition gives you pain, who hinders you from correcting your opinion? And even if you are pained because you are not doing some particular thing which seems to you to be right, why do you not rather act than complain? – But some insuperable obstacle is in the way? – Do not be grieved

then, for the cause of its not being done depends not on you. – But it is not worthwhile to live, if this cannot be done. – Take your departure then from life contentedly, just as he dies who is in full activity, and well pleased too with the things which are obstacles.

48.   Remember that the ruling faculty is invincible, when self-collected it is satisfied with itself, if it does nothing which it does not choose to do, even if it resist from mere obstinacy. What then will it be when it forms a judgment about anything aided by reason and deliberately? Therefore the mind which is free from passions is a citadel, for man has nothing more secure to which he can fly for refuge and for the future be inexpugnable. He then who has not seen this is an ignorant man but he who has seen it and does not fly to this refuge is unhappy.

49.   Say nothing more to yourself than what the first appearances report. Suppose that it has been reported to you that a certain person speaks ill of you. This has been reported but that you have been injured, that has not been reported. I see that my child is sick. I do see that, but that he is in danger I do not see. Always abide then by the first appearances, and add nothing yourself from within, and then nothing happens to you. Or rather add something like a man who knows everything that happens in the world.

50.   A cucumber is bitter. – Throw it away. – There are briers in the road. – Turn aside from them. – This is enough. Do not add, "And why were such things made in the world?" For you will be ridiculed by a man who is acquainted with nature, as you would be ridiculed by a carpenter and shoe-maker if you did find fault because you see in their workshop

shavings and cuttings from the things which they make. And yet they have places into which they can throw these shavings and cuttings, and the universal nature has no external space. But the wondrous part of her art is that though she has circumscribed herself, everything within her which appears to decay and to grow old and to be useless she changes into herself, and again makes other new things from these very same, so that she requires neither substance from without nor wants a place into which she may cast that which decays. She is content then with her own space, and her own matter, and her own art.

51.   Neither in your actions be sluggish nor in your conversation without method, nor wandering in your thoughts, nor let there be in your soul inward contention nor external effusion, nor in life be so busy as to have no leisure.

Suppose that men kill you, cut you in pieces, curse you. What then can these things do to prevent your mind from remaining pure, wise, sober, just? For instance, if a man should stand by a limpid pure spring, and curse it, the spring never ceases sending up drinkable water. And if he should cast clay into it or filth, it will speedily disperse them and wash them out, and will not be at all polluted. How then shall you possess a perpetual fountain [and not a mere well]? By forming yourself hourly to freedom conjoined with contentment, simplicity, and modesty.

52.   He who does not know what the world is, does not know where he is. And he who does not know for what purpose the world exists, does not know who he is, nor what the world is. But he who has failed in any one of these things could not even say for what purpose he exists himself. What then do you

think of him who [avoids or] seeks the praise of those who applaud, of men who know not either where they are or who they are?

53.   Do you wish to be praised by a man who curses himself thrice every hour? Would you wish to please a man who does not please himself? Does a man please himself who repents of nearly everything that he does?

54.   No longer let your breathing only act in concert with the air which surrounds you, but let your intelligence also now be in harmony with the intelligence which embraces all things. For the intelligent power is no less diffused in all parts and pervades all things for him who is willing to draw it to him than the aerial power for him who is able to respire it.

55.   Generally, wickedness does no harm at all to the universe, and particularly the wickedness [of one man] does no harm to another. It is only harmful to him who has it in his power to be released from it as soon as he shall choose.

56.   To my own free will the free will of my neighbour is just as indifferent as his poor breath and flesh. For though we are made especially for the sake of one another, still the ruling power of each of us has its own office, for otherwise my neighbour's wickedness would be my harm, which God has not willed, in order that my unhappiness may not depend on another.

57.   The sun appears to be poured down, and in all directions indeed it is diffused, yet it is not effused. For this diffusion is extension. Accordingly its rays are called extensions [ἀκτῖνες] because they are extended [ἀπὸ τοῦ ἐκτείνεσθαι]. But one may judge what kind of a thing a ray is, if he looks at the sun's light passing through a narrow opening into a

darkened room, for it is extended in a right line, and as it were is divided when it meets with any solid body which stands in the way and intercepts the air beyond. But there the light remains fixed and does not glide or fall off. Such then ought to be the outpouring and diffusion of the understanding, and it should in no way be an effusion, but an extension, and it should make no violent or impetuous collision with the obstacles which are in its way, nor yet fall down, but be fixed, and enlighten that which receives it. For a body will deprive itself of the illumination, if it does not admit it.

58.   He who fears death either fears the loss of sensation or a different kind of sensation. But if you shall have no sensation, neither will you feel any harm and if you shalt acquire another kind of sensation, you will be a different kind of living being and you will not cease to live.

59.   Men exist for the sake of one another. Teach them then, or bear with them.

60.   In one way an arrow moves, in another way the mind. The mind indeed, both when it exercises caution and when it is employed about inquiry, moves straight onward not the less, and to its object.

61.   Enter into every man's ruling faculty and also let every other man enter into yours.

BOOK NINE

1. He who acts unjustly acts impiously. For since the universal nature has made rational animals for the sake of one another, to help one another according to their deserts, but in no way to injure one another, he who transgresses her will is clearly guilty of impiety towards the highest divinity. And he too who lies is guilty of impiety to the same divinity. For the universal nature is the nature of things that are, and things that are have a relation to all things that come into existence. And further, this universal nature is named truth, and is the prime cause of all things that are true. He then who lies intentionally is guilty of impiety, inasmuch as he acts unjustly by deceiving. And he also who lies unintentionally, inasmuch as he is at variance with the universal nature, and inasmuch as he disturbs the order by fighting against the nature of the world. He fights against it, who is moved of himself to that which is contrary to truth, for he had received powers from nature through the neglect of which he is not able now to distinguish falsehood from truth. And indeed he who pursues pleasure as good, and avoids pain as evil, is guilty of impiety. For of necessity such a man must often find fault with the universal nature, alleging that it assigns things to the bad and the good contrary to their deserts, because frequently the bad are in the enjoyment of pleasure and possess the things which

procure pleasure, but the good have pain for their share and the things which cause pain. And further, he who is afraid of pain will sometimes also be afraid of some of the things which will happen in the world, and even this is impiety. And he who pursues pleasure will not abstain from injustice, and this is plainly impiety. Now with respect to the things towards which the universal nature is equally affected – for it would not have made both, unless it was equally affected towards both – towards these they who wish to follow nature should be of the same mind with it, and equally affected. With respect to pain, then, and pleasure, or death and life, or honour and dishonour, which the universal nature employs equally, who-ever is not equally affected is manifestly acting impiously. And I say that the universal nature employs them equally, instead of saying that they happen alike to those who are produced in continuous series and to those who come after them by virtue of a certain original movement of Providence, according to which it moved from a certain beginning to this ordering of things, having conceived certain principles of the things which were to be, and having determined powers productive of beings and of changes and of such like successions.

2. It would be a man's happiest lot to depart from mankind without having had any taste of lying and hypocrisy and luxury and pride. However, to breathe out one's life when a man has had enough of these things is the next best voyage, as the saying is. Have you determined to abide with vice, and has experience not yet induced you to fly from this pestilence? For the destruction of the understanding is a pestilence, much more, indeed, than any such corruption and change of

this atmosphere which surrounds us. For this corruption is a pestilence of animals so far as they are animals but the other is a pestilence of men so far as they are men.

3.   Do not despise death, but be well content with it, since this too is one of those things which nature wills. For such as it is to be young and to grow old, and to increase and to reach maturity, and to have teeth and beard and grey hairs, and to beget and to be pregnant and to bring forth, and all the other natural operations which the seasons of your life bring, such also is dissolution. This, then, is consistent with the character of a reflecting man – to be neither careless nor impatient nor contemptuous with respect to death, but to wait for it as one of the operations of nature. As you now wait for the time when the child shall come out of your wife's womb, so be ready for the time when your soul shall fall out of this envelope. But if you require also a vulgar kind of comfort which shall reach your heart, you will be made best reconciled to death by observing the objects from which you are going to be removed, and the morals of those with whom your soul will no longer be mingled. For it is no way right to be offended with men, but it is your duty to care for them and to bear with them gently, and yet to remember that your departure will not be from men who have the same principles as yourself. For this is the only thing, if there be any, which could draw us the contrary way and attach us to life – to be permitted to live with those who have the same principles as ourselves. But now you see how great is the trouble arising from the discordance of those who live together, so that you may say, "Come quick, O death, lest perchance I, too, should forget myself."

4. He who does wrong does wrong against himself. He who acts unjustly acts unjustly to himself, because he makes himself bad.

5. He often acts unjustly who does not do a certain thing, not only he who does a certain thing.

6. Your present opinion founded on understanding, and your present conduct directed to social good, and your present disposition of contentment with everything which happens – that is enough.

7. Wipe out imagination; check desire: extinguish appetite: keep the ruling faculty in its own power.

8. Among the animals which do not have reason one life is distributed but among reasonable animals one intelligent soul is distributed. Just as there is one earth of all things which are of an earthly nature, and we see by one light, and breathe one air, all of us that have the faculty of vision and all that have life.

9. All things which participate in anything which is common to them all, move towards that which is of the same kind with themselves. Everything which is earthy turns towards the earth, everything which is liquid flows together, and everything which is of an aerial kind does the same, so that they require something to keep them asunder, and the application of force. Fire indeed moves upwards on account of the elemental fire, but it is so ready to be kindled together with all the fire which is here, that even every substance which is somewhat dry is easily ignited, because there is less mingled with it of that which is a hindrance to ignition. Accordingly, then, everything also which participates in the common intelligent nature moves in

like manner towards that which is of the same kind with itself, or moves even more. For so much as it is superior in comparison with all other things, in the same degree also is it more ready to mingle with and to be fused with that which is akin to it. Accordingly among animals devoid of reason we find swarms of bees, and herds of cattle, and the nurture of young birds, and in a manner, loves. For even in animals there are souls, and that power which brings them together is seen to exert itself in a superior degree, and in such a way as never has been observed in plants nor in stones nor in trees. But in rational animals there are political communities and friendships, and families and meetings of people; and in wars, treaties, and armistices. But in the things which are still superior, even though they are separated from one another, unity in a manner exists, as in the stars. Thus the ascent to the higher degree is able to produce a sympathy even in things which are separated. See, then, what now takes place for only intelligent animals have now forgotten this mutual desire and inclination, and in them alone the property of flowing together is not seen. But still, though men strive to avoid [this union], they are caught and held by it, for their nature is too strong for them. And you will see what I say, if you only observe things. Sooner, then, will one find anything earthy which comes in contact with no earthy thing, than a man altogether separated from other men.

10.   Both man and God and the universe produce fruit; at the proper seasons each produces it. But and if usage has especially fixed these terms to the vine and like things, this is nothing. Reason produces fruit both for all and for itself, and

there are produced from it other things of the same kind as reason itself.

11.   If you are able, correct those who do wrong by teaching them. But if you cannot, remember that indulgence is given to you for this purpose. And the gods, too, are indulgent to such persons. For some purposes they even help them to get health, wealth, reputation; so kind they are. And it is in your power also or else who hinders you?

12.   Do not labour as if you were wretched, nor yet as though you should be pitied or admired but direct your will to one thing only: to put yourself in motion and to check yourself, as the social reason requires.

13.   Today I have got out of all trouble, or rather I have cast out all trouble, for it was not outside, but within and in my opinions.

14.   All things are the same, familiar in experience, and ephemeral in time, and worthless in the matter. Everything now is just as it was in the time of those whom we have buried.

15.   Things stand outside of us, themselves by themselves, neither knowing aught of themselves, nor expressing any judgment. What is it, then, which does judge about them? The ruling faculty.

16.   Not in passivity but in activity lie the evil and the good of the rational social animal, just as his virtue and his vice lie not in passivity but in activity.

17.   For the stone which has been thrown up it is no evil to come down, nor indeed any good to have been carried up.

18.   Penetrate inwards into men's leading principles, and you will see of what judges you are afraid, and what kind of judges they are of themselves.

19.   All things are changing: and you yourself are in continuous mutation and in a manner in continuous destruction, and the whole universe too.

20.   It is your duty to leave another man's wrongful act there where it is.

21.   Termination of activity, cessation from movement and opinion, and in a sense their death, is no evil. Turn your thoughts now to the consideration of your life, your life as a child, as a youth, your manhood, your old age, for in these also every change was a death. Is this anything to fear? Turn your thoughts now to your life under your grandfather, then to your life under your mother, then to your life under your father; and as you find many other differences and changes and terminations, ask yourself, "Is this anything to fear?" In like manner, then, neither are the termination and cessation and change of your whole life things of which you should be afraid.

22.   Hasten [to examine] your own ruling faculty and that of the universe and that of your neighbour: your own, that you may make it just: and that of the universe, that you may remember of what you are a part; and that of your neighbour, that you may know whether he has acted ignorantly or with knowledge, and you may also consider that his ruling faculty is akin to your own.

23.   As you yourself art a component part of a social system, so let every act of yours be a component part of social life. Whatever act of yours then has no reference either immediately or remotely to a social end, this tears asunder your life,

and does not allow it to be one, and it is of the nature of a mutiny, just as when in a popular assembly a man acting by himself stands apart from the general agreement.

24. Quarrels of little children and their sports, and poor spirits carrying about dead bodies [such is everything]. And so what is exhibited in the representation of the mansions of the dead strikes our eyes more clearly.

25. Examine the quality of the form of an object, and detach it altogether from its material part, and then contemplate it. Then determine the time, the longest which a thing of this peculiar form is naturally made to endure.

26. You have endured infinite troubles through not being contented with your ruling faculty when it does the things which it is constituted by nature to do. But enough [of this].

27. When another blames you or hates you, or when men say about you anything injurious, approach their poor souls, penetrate within, and see what kind of men they are. You will discover that there is no reason to take any trouble that these men may have this or that opinion about you. However, you must be well disposed towards them, for by nature they are friends. And the gods too aid them in all ways, by dreams, by signs, towards the attainment of those things on which they set a value.

28. The periodic movements of the universe are the same, up and down from age to age. And either the universal intelligence puts itself in motion for every separate effect, and if this is so, be content with that which is the result of its activity; or it puts itself in motion once, and everything else comes by way of sequence in a manner; or indivisible elements are

the origin of all things. In a word, if there is a god, all is well; and if chance rules, do not also be governed by it yourself.

Soon the earth will cover us all then the earth too will change. And the things also which result from change will continue to change forever, and these again forever. For if a man reflects on the changes and transformations which follow one another like wave after wave and their rapidity, he will despise everything which is perishable.

29.   The universal cause is like a winter torrent: it carries everything along with it. But how worthless are all these pathetic individuals who are engaged in matters political and suppose they are playing the part of a philosopher! All drivellers. Well then, man, do what nature now requires. Set yourself in motion, if it is in your power, and do not look about yourself to see if anyone will observe it. Nor yet expect Plato's Republic: but be content if the smallest thing goes on well, and consider such an event to be no small matter. For who can change men's opinions? And without a change of opinions what else is there than the slavery of men who groan while they pretend to obey? Come now and tell me of Alexander the Great and Philippus and Demetrius of Phalerum. They themselves shall judge whether they discovered what the common nature required, and trained themselves accordingly. But if they acted like tragic heroes, no one has condemned me to imitate them. Simple and modest is the work of philosophy. Do not draw me aside to insolence and pride.

30.   Look down from above on the countless herds of men and their countless rituals, and the infinitely varied voyages in storms and calms, and the differences among those who are born, who live together, and die. And consider, too, the life

lived by others in olden times, and the life of those who will live after you, and the life now lived among barbarous nations. And how many do not even know your name, and how many will soon forget it, and how they who perhaps now are praising you will very soon blame you, and that neither a posthumous name is of any value, nor reputation, nor anything else.

31.   Let there be freedom from perturbation with respect to the things which come from the external cause and let there be justice in the things done by virtue of the internal cause, that is, let there be movement and action terminating in this, in social acts, for this is according to your nature.

32.   You can remove out of the way many useless things among those which disturb you, for they lie entirely in your opinion and you will then gain for yourself ample space by comprehending the whole universe in your mind, and by contemplating the eternity of time, and observing the rapid change of every several thing, how short is the time from birth to dissolution, and the illimitable time before birth as well as the equally boundless time after dissolution!

33.   All that you see will quickly perish, and those who have been spectators of its dissolution will very soon perish too. And he who dies at the most extreme old age will be brought to the same condition as one who died prematurely.

34.   What are these men's leading principles, and about what kind of things are they busy, and for what kind of reasons do they love and honour? Imagine that you see their poor souls laid bare. When they think that they do harm by their blame or good by their praise – what a ridiculous idea!

35.   Loss is nothing else than change. But the universal nature delights in change, and in obedience to her all things

are now done well, and from eternity have been in like form, and will be such to time without end. What, then, do you say – that all things have been and all things always will be bad, and that no power has ever been found in so many gods to rectify these things, but the world has been condemned to be bound in never ceasing evil?

36.   The rottenness of the matter which is the foundation of everything! Water, dust, bones, filth: or again, marble rocks, the callosities of the earth; and gold and silver, the sediments; and garments, only bits of hair; and purple dye, blood; and everything else is of the same kind. And that which is of the nature of breath is also another thing of the same kind, changing from this to that.

37.   Enough of this wretched life and murmuring and apish tricks. Why are you disturbed? What is there new in this? What unsettles you? Is it the form of the thing? Look at it. Or is it the matter? Look at it. But besides these there is nothing. Towards the gods then, now become at last simpler and better. It is the same whether we examine these things for a hundred years or three.

38.   If a man has done wrong the harm is his own. But perhaps he has not done wrong.

39.   Either all things proceed from one intelligent source and come together as in one body, and the part ought not to find fault with what is done for the benefit of the whole; or there are only atoms, and nothing else than mixture and dispersion. Why, then, are you disturbed? Say to the ruling faculty, "Are you dead, are you corrupted, are you acting hypocritically, are you turning into a beast, do you herd and feed with the rest?"

40.   Either the gods have no power or they have power. If, then, they have no power, why do you pray to them? But if they have power, why do you not pray for them to give you the faculty of not fearing any of the things which you fear, or of not desiring any of the things which you desire, or not being pained at anything, rather than pray that any of these things should or should not happen? For certainly if they can cooperate with men, they can cooperate for these purposes. But perhaps you will say the gods have placed them in your power. Well, then, is it not better to use what is in your power like a free man than to desire in a slavish and abject way what is not in your power? And who has told you that the gods do not aid us, even in the things which are in our power? Begin, then, to pray for such things, and you will see. One man prays thus: "How shall I be able to lie with that woman?" You should pray like this: "How shall I not desire to lie with her?" Another prays thus: "How shall I be released from this?" You should pray: "How shall I not desire to be released?" Another thus: "How shall I not lose my little son?" You: "How shall I not be afraid to lose him?" Indeed, turn your prayers this way, and see what comes of it.

41.   Epicurus says, "In my sickness my conversation was not about my bodily sufferings, nor," says he, "did I talk on such subjects to those who visited me; but I continued to discourse on the nature of things as before, keeping to this main point, how the mind, while participating in such movements as go on in the poor flesh, shall be free from perturbations and maintain its proper good." "Nor did I," he says, "give the physicians an opportunity of putting on solemn looks, as if they were doing something great, but my life went on well and happily."

Do, then, the same that he did both in sickness, if you are sick, and in any other circumstances. For never to desert philosophy in any events that may befall us, nor to hold trifling talks either with an ignorant man or with one unacquainted with nature, is a principle of all schools of philosophy but to be intent only on that which you are now doing and on the instrument by which you do it.

42. When you are offended with any man's shameless conduct, immediately ask yourself, "Is it possible, then, that shameless men should not be in the world?" It is not possible. Do not, then, require what is impossible. For this man also is one of those shameless men who must of necessity be in the world. Let the same considerations be present to your mind in the case of the knave, and the faithless man, and of every man who does wrong in any way. For at the same time that you dost remind yourself that it is impossible that such kind of men should not exist, you will become more kindly disposed towards everyone individually. It is useful to perceive this, too, immediately when the occasion arises, what virtue nature has given to man to oppose to every wrongful act. For she has given to man, as an antidote against the stupid man, mildness, and against another kind of man some other power. And in all cases it is possible for you to correct by teaching the man who is gone astray; for every man who errs misses his object and is gone astray. Besides, wherein have you been injured? For you will find that no one among those against whom you are irritated has done anything by which your mind could be made worse but that which is evil to you and harmful has its foundation only in the mind. And what harm is done or what is there strange, if the man who has not been instructed does

the acts of an uninstructed man? Consider whether you should not rather blame yourself, because you did not expect such a man to err in such a way. For you had means given you by your reason to suppose that it was likely that he would commit this error, and yet you have forgotten and are amazed that he has erred. But most of all when you blame a man as faithless or ungrateful, turn to yourself. For the fault is manifestly your own, whether you did trust that a man who had such a disposition would keep his promise, or when conferring your kindness you did not confer it absolutely, nor yet in such a way as to have received from your very act all the profit. For what more do you want when you have done a man a service? Are you not content that you have done something conformable to your nature, and do you seek to be paid for it? It is just as if the eye demanded a recompense for seeing, or the feet for walking. For as these members are formed for a particular purpose, and by working according to their several constitutions obtain what is their own so also as man is formed by nature to acts of benevolence, when he has done anything benevolent or in any other way conducive to the common interest, he has acted conformably to his constitution, and he gets what is his own.

BOOK TEN

1. Will you, then, my soul, never be good and simple and one and naked, more manifest than the body which surrounds you? Will you never enjoy an affectionate and contented disposition? Will you never be full and without a want of any kind, longing for nothing more, nor desiring anything, either animate or inanimate, for the enjoyment of pleasures? Nor yet desiring time wherein you shall have longer enjoyment, or place, or pleasant climate, or society of men with whom you may live in harmony? But will you be satisfied with your present condition, and pleased with all that is about you. And will you convince yourself that you have everything, and that it comes from the gods. And that everything is well for you, and will be well whatever shall please them, and whatever they shall give for the conservation of the perfect living being, the good and just and beautiful, which generates and holds together all things, and contains and embraces all things which are dissolved for the production of other like things? Will you never be such that you shall so dwell in community with gods and men as neither to find fault with them at all, nor to be condemned by them?

2. Observe what your nature requires, so far as you are governed by nature only. Then do it and accept it, if your nature, so far as you are a living being, shall not be made worse by it. And next you must observe what your nature requires so

far as you are a living being. And all this you may allow yourself, if your nature, so far as you are a rational animal, shall not be made worse by it. But the rational animal is consequently also a political [social] animal. Use these rules, then, and trouble yourself about nothing else.

3. Everything which happens either happens in such ways as you are formed by nature to bear, or as you are not formed by nature to bear. If, then, it happens to you in such a way as you are formed by nature to bear, do not complain, but bear it as you are formed by nature to bear it. But if it happens in such ways as you are not formed by nature to bear, do not complain, for it will perish after it has consumed you. Remember, however, that you are formed by nature to bear everything, with respect to which it depends on your own opinion to make it endurable and tolerable, by thinking that it is either your interest or your duty to do this.

4. If a man is mistaken, instruct him kindly and show him his error. But if you are not able, blame yourself, or do not blame even yourself.

5. Whatever may happen to you, it was prepared for you from all eternity; and the implication of causes was from eternity spinning the thread of your being, and of that which is incidental to it.

6. Whether the universe is [a random collision of] atoms, or nature [as an ordered system], let this be established first: that I am a part of the whole which is governed by nature; next, I am in a manner intimately related to the parts which are of the same kind as myself. For remembering this, inasmuch as I am a part, I shall be discontented with none of the things which are assigned to me out of the whole; for nothing

is injurious to the part if it is for the advantage of the whole. For the whole contains nothing which is not for its advantage. And all natures indeed have this common principle, but the nature of the universe has this principle besides, that it cannot be compelled even by any external cause to generate anything harmful to itself. By remembering, then, that I am a part of such a whole, I shall be content with everything that happens. And inasmuch as I am in a manner intimately related to the parts which are of the same kind with myself, I shall do nothing unsocial, but I shall rather direct myself to the things which are of the same kind with myself, and I shall turn all my efforts to the common interest, and divert them from the contrary. Now, if these things are done so, life must flow on happily, just as you may observe that the life of a citizen is happy, who continues a course of action which is advantageous to his fellow citizens, and is content with whatever the state may assign to him.

7. The parts of the whole, everything, I mean, which is naturally comprehended in the universe, must of necessity perish. Let this be understood in this sense: that they must undergo change. But if this were naturally both an evil and a necessity for the parts, the whole would not continue to exist in a good condition, the parts being subject to change and constituted so as to perish in various ways. For whether Nature herself designed to do evil to the things which are parts of herself, and to make them subject to evil and of necessity fall into evil, or whether she had such results happen without her knowing it, both these suppositions, indeed, are incredible. But if a man should even drop the term Nature [as an efficient power], and should speak of these things as natural, even then it would be

ridiculous to affirm at the same time that the parts of the whole are in their nature subject to change, and at the same time to be surprised or vexed as if something were happening contrary to nature, particularly as the dissolution of things is into those things of which each thing is composed. For there is either a dispersion of the elements out of which everything has been compounded, or a change from the solid to the earthy and from the airy to the aerial, so that these parts are taken back into the universal reason, whether this at certain periods is consumed by fire or renewed by eternal changes. And do not imagine that the solid and the airy part belong to you from the time of generation. For all this received its accretion only yesterday and the day before, as one may say, from the food and the air which is inspired. This, then, which has received [the accretion], changes, not that which your mother brought forth. But suppose that this [which your mother brought forth] implicates you very much with that other part, which has the peculiar quality [of change], this is nothing in fact in the way of objection to what is said.

8. When you have assumed these names, good, modest, true, rational, a man of equanimity, and magnanimous, take care that you dost not change them; and if you should lose them, quickly return to them. Remember that the term "Rational" was intended to signify a discriminating attention to every individual thing, and freedom from negligence; and that "Equanimity" is the voluntary acceptance of the things which are assigned to you by the common nature; and that "Magnanimity" is the elevation of the intelligent part above the pleasurable or painful sensations of the flesh, and above that poor thing called fame, and death, and all such things. If,

then, you maintain yourself in the possession of these names, without desiring to be called by these names by others, you will be another person and will enter on another life. For to continue to be such as you have previously been, and to be torn to pieces and defiled in such a life, is the character of a very stupid man and one overly-fond of his life, like those half-devoured fighters with wild beasts, who though covered with wounds and gore, still beg to be kept to the following day, though they will be exposed in the same state to the same claws and bites. Therefore fix yourself in the possession of these few names: and if you are able to abide in them, abide as if you were removed to the Isles of the Blessed. But if you shall perceive that you fall out of them and do not maintain your hold, go courageously into some nook where you shall maintain them, or even depart at once from life, not in passion, but with simplicity and freedom and modesty, after doing this one [laudable] thing at least in your life, to have gone out of it thus. In order, however, to remember these names it will greatly help you if you remember the gods, and that they do not wish to be flattered but for all reasonable beings to be made like themselves. And if you remember that what does the work of a fig-tree is a fig-tree, and that what does the work of a dog is a dog, and that what does the work of a bee is a bee, and that what does the work of a man is a man.

9. Hatred, war, astonishment, torpor, slavery, will daily wipe out those holy principles of yours. How many things without studying nature do you imagine, and how many do you neglect? But it is your duty so to look on and so to do everything, that at the same time the power of dealing with circumstances is perfected, and the contemplative faculty is exercised,

and the confidence which comes from the knowledge of each individual thing is maintained without showing it, but yet not concealed. For when will you enjoy simplicity, when gravity, and when the knowledge of every individual thing, both what it is in substance, and what place it has in the universe, and how long it is formed to exist, and of what things it is compounded, and to whom it can belong, and who are able both to give it and take it away?

10. A spider is proud when it has caught a fly, and another when he has caught a poor hare, and another when he has taken a little fish in a net, and another when he has taken wild boars, and another when he has taken bears, and another when he has captured Sarmatians. Are these not robbers, if you examine their opinions?

11. Acquire the contemplative way of seeing how all things change into one another, and constantly attend to it, and exercise yourself about this part [of philosophy]. For nothing is so much adapted to produce magnanimity. Such a man has put off the body, and as he sees that he must, no one knows how soon, go away from among men and leave everything here, he gives himself up entirely to just doing in all his actions, and in everything else that happens he resigns himself to the universal nature. But as to what any man shall say or think about him or do against him, he never even thinks of it, being himself contented with these two things: acting justly in what he now does, and being satisfied with what is now assigned to him. And he lays aside all distracting and busy pursuits, and desires nothing else than to accomplish the straight course through the law and by accomplishing the straight course to follow God.

12.   What need is there of suspicious fear, since it is in your power to inquire what ought to be done? And if you see clearly, go by this way content, without turning back; but if you do not see clearly, stop and take the best advisers. But if any other things oppose you, go on according to your powers with due consideration, keeping to that which appears to be just. For it is best to reach this object, and if you do fail, let your failure be in attempting this. He who follows reason in all things is both tranquil and active at the same time, and also cheerful and collected.

13.   Inquire of yourself as soon as you awaken from sleep whether it will make any difference to you if another does what is just and right. It will make no difference.

You have not forgotten, I suppose, that those who assume arrogant airs in bestowing their praise or blame on others are such as they are at bed and at board, and you have not forgotten what they do, and what they avoid, and what they pursue, and how they steal and how they rob, not with hands and feet, but with their most valuable part, by means of which there is produced, when a man chooses, fidelity, modesty, truth, law, a good daemon [happiness]?

14.   To her who gives and takes back all, to nature, the man who is instructed and modest says, "Give what you will; take back what you will." And he says this not proudly, but obediently, and well pleased with her.

15.   Short is the little which remains to you of life. Live as on a mountain. For it makes no difference whether a man lives there or here, if he lives everywhere in the world as in a state [political community]. Let me see, let them know a real man who lives according to nature. If they cannot endure

him, let them kill him. For that is better than to live thus [as men do].

16.   No longer talk at all about the kind of man that a good man ought to be, but be such.

17.   Constantly contemplate the whole of time and the whole of substance, and consider that all individual things as to substance are a grain of a fig, and as to time the turning of a screw.

18.   Look at everything that exists, and observe that it is already in dissolution and in change, and as it were putre-faction or dispersion, or that everything is so constituted by nature as to die.

19.   Consider what men are when they are eating, sleep-ing, generating, relieving themselves, and so forth. Then what kind of men they are when they are imperious and arrogant, or angry and scolding from their elevated place. But a short time ago to how many they were slaves and for what things, and after a little time consider in what a condition they will be.

20.   That is for the good of each thing, which the universal nature brings to each. And it is for its good at the time when nature brings it.

21.   "The earth loves the shower"; and "the solemn ether loves"; and the universe loves to make whatever is about to be. I say then to the universe, that I love as you love. And is not this too said that "this or that loves [tends] to be produced?"

22.   Either you live here and have already accustomed yourself to it, or you are going away, and this was your own will; or you are dying and have discharged your duty. But besides these things there is nothing. Be of good cheer, then.

23.   Let this always be plain to you, that this piece of land is like any other, and that all things here are the same with things on the top of a mountain, or on the seashore, or wherever you choose to be. For you will find just what Plato says, "Dwelling within the walls of a city as in a shepherd's fold on a mountain."

24.   What is my ruling faculty now to me? And of what nature am I now making it? And for what purpose am I now using it? Is it void of understanding? Is it lost and rent asunder from social life? Is it melted into and mixed with the poor flesh so as to move together with it?

25.   He who flees from his master is a runaway but the law is master so he who breaks the law is a runaway. And he also who is grieved or angry or afraid is dissatisfied because of something that has been or is or shall be of the things which are appointed by Him who rules all things, and he is Law and assigns to every man what is fit. He then who fears or is grieved or is angry is a runaway.

26.   A man deposits seed in a womb and goes away, and then another cause takes it and labours on it, and makes a child. What a thing from such a material! Again, the child passes food down through the throat, and then another cause takes it and makes perception and motion, and indeed, life and strength and other things. How many and how strange! Observe then the things which are produced in such a hidden way, and see the power, just as we see the power which carries things downwards and upwards, not with the eyes, but still no less plainly.

27.   Constantly consider how all things such as they now are, in time past also were; and consider that they will be the same again. And place before your eyes entire dramas

and stages of the same form, whatever you have learned from your experience or from older history. For example, the whole court of Hadrian, and the whole court of Antoninus, and the whole court of Philippus, Alexander the Great, Croesus; for all those were such dramas as we see now, only with different actors.

28.   Imagine every man who is grieved at anything or discontented to be like a pig which is sacrificed and kicks and screams.

Like this pig also is he who on his bed in silence laments the bonds in which we are held. And consider that only to the rational animal is it given to follow voluntarily what happens but simply to follow is a necessity imposed on all.

29.   On the occasion of every individual thing that you do, pause and ask yourself if death is a dreadful thing because it deprives you of this.

30.   When you are offended at any man's fault, immediately turn to yourself and reflect in what manner you err yourself. For example, in thinking that money is a good thing, or pleasure, or a bit of reputation, and the like. For by attending to this you will quickly forget your anger, if this consideration also is added, that the man is compelled: for what else could he do? Or, if you are able, take away from him the compulsion.

31.   When you see Satyron the Socratic, think of either Eutyches or Hymen, and when you see Euphrates, think of Eutychion or Silvanus, and when you see Alciphron think of Tropaeophorus, and when you see Xenophon, think of Crito or Severus, and when you look on yourself, think of any other Caesar, and in the case of everyone else do the same thing.

Then let this thought be in your mind, "Where then are those men now?" Nowhere, or nobody knows where. For thereby you will continuously look at human things as smoke and nothing at all, especially if you reflect at the same time that what has once changed will never exist again in the infinite duration of time. But you, in what a brief space of time is your existence? And why are you not content to pass through this short time in an orderly way? What matter and opportunity [for your activity] are you avoiding? For what else are all these things, except exercises for the reason, when it has viewed carefully and by examination into their nature the things which happen in life? Persevere then until you shall have made these things your own, as the stomach which is strengthened makes all things its own, as the blazing fire makes flame and brightness out of everything that is thrown into it.

32. Let it not be in any man's power to say truly of you that you are not simple or that you are not good; but let him be a liar whoever shall think anything of this kind about you and this is altogether in your power. For who is he that shall hinder you from being good and simple? Determine to live no longer unless you shall be so. For neither does reason allow [you to live], if you are not so.

33. What is that which can be done or said in the way most conformable to reason regarding this material [our life]? For whatever this may be, it is in your power to do it or to say it, and do not make excuses that you are hindered. You will not cease to lament until your mind is in such a condition that what luxury is to those who enjoy pleasure, such shall be to you, in the matter which is subjected and presented to

you, the doing of the things which are conformable to man's constitution. For a man ought to consider as an enjoyment everything which it is in his power to do according to his own nature. And it is in his power everywhere. Now, it is not given to a cylinder to move everywhere by its own motion, nor yet to water nor to fire, nor to anything else which is governed by nature or an irrational soul, for the things which check them and stand in the way are many. But intelligence and reason are able to go through everything that opposes them, and in such manner as they are formed by nature and as they choose. Place before your eyes this facility with which the reason will be carried through all things, as fire upwards, as a stone downwards, as a cylinder down an inclined surface, and seek for nothing further. For all other obstacles either affect the body only, which is a dead thing or, except through opinion and the yielding of the reason itself, they do not crush nor do any harm of any kind. For if they did, he who felt it would immediately become bad. Now, in the case of all things which have a certain constitution, whatever harm may happen to any of them, that which is so affected becomes consequently worse. But in the like case, a man becomes both better, if one may say so, and more worthy of praise by making a right use of these accidents. And finally remember that nothing harms him who is really a citizen, which does not harm the state nor yet does anything harm the state, which does not harm law [order]. And of these things which are called misfortunes not one harms law. What then does not harm law does not harm either state or citizen.

34. To him who is penetrated by true principles even the briefest precept is sufficient, and any common precept, to

remind him that he should be free from grief and fear. For example:

"Leaves, some the wind scatters on the ground
So is the race of men."

Leaves, also, are your children. And leaves, too, are they who cry out as if they were worthy of credit and bestow their praise, or on the contrary curse, or secretly blame and sneer. And leaves, in like manner, are those who shall receive and transmit a man's fame to after-times. For all such things as these "are produced in the season of spring," as the poet says. Then the wind casts them down and the forest produces other leaves in their places. But a brief existence is common to all things, and yet you avoid and pursue all things as if they would be eternal. A little time, and you shall close your eyes and soon another will lament him who has attended you to your grave.

35.   The healthy eye ought to see all visible things and not say, "I wish for green things." For this is the condition of a diseased eye. And the healthy hearing and smelling ought to be ready to perceive all that can be heard and smelled. And the healthy stomach ought to be with respect to all food just as the mill with respect to all things which it is formed to grind. And accordingly the healthy understanding ought to be prepared for everything which happens but that which says, "Let my dear children live, and let all men praise whatever I may do," is an eye which seeks for green things, or teeth which seek for soft things.

36.   There is no man so fortunate that there shall not be by him when he is dying some who are pleased with what is going to happen. Suppose that he was a good and wise man,

will there not be at least someone to say to himself, "Let us at last breathe freely, being relieved from this schoolmaster? It is true that he was harsh to none of us, but I perceived that he tacitly condemns us." This is what is said of a good man. But in your own case how many other things are there for which there are many who wish to get rid of you? You will consider this, then, when you are dying, and you will depart more contentedly by reflecting thus: "I am going away from such a life, in which even my associates in behalf of whom I have striven so much, prayed, and cared, themselves wish me to depart, hoping perchance to get some little advantage by it." Why then should a man cling to a longer stay here? Do not, however, for this reason go away less kindly disposed to them, but preserving your own character, and friendly and benevolent and mild, and on the other hand not as if you were torn away but as when a man dies a quiet death, the poor soul is easily separated from the body, such also ought your departure from men be for nature united you to them and associated you. But does she now dissolve the union? Well, I am separated as from kinsmen, not however dragged resisting, but without compulsion for this, too, is one of the things according to nature.

37.   Accustom yourself as much as possible on the occasion of anything being done by any person to inquire with yourself, "For what object is this man doing this?" But begin with yourself, and examine yourself first.

38.   Remember that this which pulls the strings is the thing which is hidden within: this is the power of persuasion, this is life, this, if one may so say, is man. In contemplating yourself never include the vessel which surrounds you and these instruments which are attached about it. For they are like an

axe, differing only in this, that they grow on the body. For indeed there is no more use in these parts without the cause which moves and checks them than in the weaver's shuttle, and the writer's pen, and the driver's whip.

BOOK ELEVEN

1.   These are the properties of the rational soul: it sees itself, analyses itself, and makes itself such as it chooses. The fruit which it bears it enjoys itself – for the fruits of plants and that in animals which corresponds to fruits others enjoy. It obtains its own end wherever the limit of life may be fixed. Not as in a dance and in a play and in such like things, where the whole action is incomplete if anything cuts it short but in every part. And wherever it may be stopped it makes what has been set before it full and complete so that it can say, "I have what is my own." And further it traverses the whole universe, and the surrounding vacuum, and surveys its form, and it extends itself into the infinity of time, and embraces and comprehends the periodical renovation of all things. And it comprehends that those who come after us will see nothing new, nor have those before us seen anything more, but in a manner he who is forty years old, if he has any understanding at all, has seen by virtue of the uniformity that prevails all things which have been and all that will be. This too is a property of the rational soul, love of one's neighbour, and truth and modesty. And to value nothing more than itself, which is also the property of Law. Thus the right reason differs not at all from the reason of justice.

2.   You will set little value on pleasant song and dance and the pancratium if you will separate the melody of the voice into

its individual sounds and ask yourself regarding each if you are mastered by this. For you will be prevented by shame from confessing it. And in the matter of dancing, if at each movement and attitude you will do the same; and the same also in the matter of the pancratium. In all things, then, except virtue and the acts of virtue, remember to apply yourself to their individual parts, and by this division to come to value them little. Apply this rule also to your whole life.

3. What a soul that is which is ready, if at any moment it must be separated from the body, and ready either to be extinguished or dispersed or continue to exist. But so that this readiness comes from a man's own judgment, not from mere obstinacy, as with the Christians, but considerately and with dignity and in a way to persuade another, without tragic show.

4. Have I done something for the general interest? Well then, I have had my reward. Let this always be present to your mind, and never stop [doing such good].

5. What is your art? To be good. And how is this accomplished well except by general principles, some about the nature of the universe, and others about the proper constitution of man?

6. At first tragedies were brought on the stage as means of reminding men of the things which happen to them, and that it is according to nature for things to happen so, and that, if you are delighted with what is shown on the stage, you should not be troubled with that which takes place on the larger stage. For you see that these things must be accomplished thus, and that even they bear them who cry out, "O Cithaeron." And,

indeed, some things are said well by the dramatic writers, of which kind is the following especially:

"Me and my children if the gods neglect,
This has its reason too."
And again,
"We must not chafe and fret at that which happens."
And,
"Life's harvest reap like the wheat's fruitful ear."
And other things of the same kind.

After tragedy the old comedy was introduced, which had a magisterial freedom of speech, and by its very plainness of speaking was useful in reminding men to beware of insolence and for this purpose too Diogenes used to take from these writers.

But as to the middle comedy, which came next, observe what it was, and again, for what object the new comedy was introduced, which gradually sank down into a mere mimic artifice. That some good things are said even by these writers, everybody knows but the whole plan of such poetry and dramaturgy, to what end does it look?

7. How plain does it appear that there is not another condition of life so well suited for philosophizing as this in which you now happen to be.

8. A branch cut off from the adjacent branch must of necessity be cut off from the whole tree also. So too a man when he is separated from another man has fallen off from the whole social community. Now as to a branch, another cuts it off but a man by his own act separates himself from his

neighbour when he hates him and turns away from him and he does not know that he has at the same time cut himself off from the whole social system. Yet he has this privilege certainly from Zeus, who framed society, for it is in our power to grow again to that which is near to us, and again to become a part which helps to make up the whole. However, if it often happens, this kind of separation, it makes it difficult for that which detaches itself to be brought to unity and to be restored to its former condition. Finally, the branch, which from the first grew together with the tree, and has continued to have one life with it, is not like that which after being cut off is then ingrafted, for this is something like what the gardeners mean when they say that it grows with the rest of the tree, but that it has not the same mind with it.

9. As those who try to stand in your way when you are proceeding according to right reason will not be able to turn you aside from your proper action, so neither let them drive you from your benevolent feelings toward them, but be on your guard equally in both matters, not only in the matter of steady judgment and action, but also in the matter of gentleness to those who try to hinder or otherwise trouble you. For this also is a weakness, to be vexed at them, as well as to be diverted from your course of action and to give way through fear. For both are equally deserters from their post: the man who does it through fear and the man who is alienated from him who is by nature a kinsman and a friend.

10. There is no nature which is inferior to art, for the arts imitate the natures of things. But if this is so, that nature which is the most perfect and the most comprehensive of all

natures, cannot fall short of the skill of art. Now all arts do the inferior things for the sake of the superior. Therefore the universal nature does so too. And, indeed, hence is the origin of justice, and in justice the other virtues have their foundation. For justice will not be observed, if we either care for middle things [things indifferent], or are easily deceived and careless and changeable.

11.   If the things do not come to you, the pursuits and avoidances of which disturb you, still in a manner you go to them. Then let your judgment about them be at rest, and they will remain quiet, and you will not be seen either pursuing or avoiding.

12.   The spherical form of the soul maintains its figure when it is neither extended towards any object, nor contracted inwards, nor dispersed, nor sinks down, but is illuminated by light, by which it sees the truth – the truth of all things and the truth that is in itself.

13.   Suppose any man shall despise me. Let him look to that himself. But I will look to it that I am not discovered doing or saying anything deserving of contempt. Shall any man hate me? Let him look to it. But I will be mild and benevolent towards every man, and ready to show even him his mistake, not reproachfully, nor yet as making a display of my endurance, but nobly and honestly, like the great Phocion, unless indeed he only assumed it. For the interior [parts] ought to be such, and a man ought to be seen by the gods neither dissatisfied with anything nor complaining. For what evil is it to you, if you are now doing what is agreeable to your own nature, and art satisfied with that which at this moment is suitable to the nature of the universe, since you are a human

being placed at your post in order that what is for the common advantage may be done in some way?

14.   Men despise one another and flatter one another and men wish to raise themselves above one another, and crouch before one another.

15.   How unsound and insincere is he who says, "I have determined to deal with you in a fair way!" What are you doing, man? There is no occasion to give this notice. It will soon show itself by acts. The voice ought to be plainly written on the forehead. Such as a man's character is, he immediately shows it in his eyes, just as he who is beloved immediately reads everything in the eyes of lovers. The man who is honest and good ought to be exactly like a man who smells strong, so that the bystander as soon as he comes near him must smell whether he chooses to or not. But the affectation of honesty is like a crooked stick. Nothing is more disgraceful than a wolfish friendship [false friendship]. Avoid this most of all. The good and honest and benevolent show all these things in the eyes, and there is no mistaking.

16.   As to living in the best way, this power is in the soul, if it be indifferent to things which are indifferent. And it will be indifferent, if it looks on each of these things separately and all together, and if it remembers that not one of them produces in us an opinion about itself, nor comes to us. But these things remain immovable, and it is we ourselves who produce the judgments about them, and, as we may say, write them in ourselves, it being in our power not to write them, and it being in our power, if perchance these judgments have imperceptibly got admission to our minds, to wipe them out. And if we remember also that such attention will only be for a short time,

and then life will be at an end. Besides, what trouble is there at all in doing this? For if these things are according to nature, rejoice in them and they will be easy to you. But if contrary to nature, seek what is conformable to your own nature, and strive towards this, even if it brings no reputation for every man is allowed to seek his own good.

17. Consider from where each thing has come, and of what it consists, and into what it changes, and what kind of thing it will be when it has changed, and that it will sustain no harm thereby.

18. [If any have offended against you, consider first]: What is my relation to men, and that we are made for one another. And in another respect I was made to be set over them, as a ram over the flock or a bull over the herd. But examine the matter from first principles, from this. If all things are not mere atoms, it is nature which orders all things. If this is so, the inferior things exist for the sake of the superior, and these for the sake of one another.

Second, consider what kind of men they are at their table, in bed, and so forth. And particularly, under what compulsions in respect of opinions they are. And as to their acts, consider with what pride they do what they do.

Third, that if men do rightly what they do, we ought not to be displeased. But if they do not do right, it is plain that they do so involuntarily and in ignorance. For as every soul is unwillingly deprived of the truth, so also is it unwillingly deprived of the power of behaving to each man according to his deserts. Accordingly men are pained when they are called unjust, ungrateful, and greedy, and in a word wrongdoers to their neighbours.

Fourth, consider that you also do many things wrong, and that you are a man like others. And even if you do abstain from certain faults, still you have the disposition to commit them, even if through cowardice, or concern about reputation, or some such mean motive, you do abstain from such faults.

Fifth, consider that you do not even understand whether men are doing wrong or not, for many things are done with a certain reference to circumstances. And in short, a man must learn a great deal to enable him to pass a correct judgment on another man's acts.

Sixth, consider when you are very frustrated or aggrieved, that man's life is only a moment, and after a short time we are all laid out dead.

Seventh, that it is not men's acts which disturb us, for those acts have their foundation in men's ruling principles, but it is our own opinions which disturb us. Take away these opinions then, and resolve to dismiss your judgment about an act as if it were something grievous, and your anger is gone. How then shall I take away these opinions? By reflecting that no wrongful act of another brings shame on you. For unless that which is shameful alone is bad you must also necessarily do many things wrong and become a robber and everything else.

Eighth, consider how much more pain is brought on us by the anger and frustration caused by such acts than by the acts themselves, at which we are angry and frustrated.

Ninth, consider that a good disposition is invincible if it is genuine, and not an affected smile and acting a part. For what will the most violent man do to you, if you continue to be of a kind disposition towards him, and if, as opportunity offers, you gently admonish him and calmly correct his errors at the very time when he is trying to do you harm, saying, "Not so, my child; we are constituted by nature for something else; I shall certainly not be injured, but you art injuring yourself, my child." And show him with gentle tact and by general principles that this is so, and that even bees do not do as he does, nor any animals which are formed by nature to be gregarious. And you must do this neither with any double meaning nor in the way of reproach, but affectionately and without any rancour in your soul. And not as if you were lecturing him nor yet that any bystander may admire, either when he is alone or if others are present...

Remember these nine rules, as if you had received them as a gift from the Muses, and begin at last to be a man while you live. But you must equally avoid lecturing men and being frustrated at them, for both are unsocial and lead to harm. And let this truth be present to you in the excitement of anger: that to be moved by passion is not manly but that mildness and gentleness, as they are more agreeable to human nature, are more manly. And he who possesses these qualities possesses strength, nerves, and courage, and not the man who is subject to fits of passion and discontent. For in the same degree to the extent that a man's mind is nearer to freedom from all passion it is also nearer to strength. And as the sense of pain is a characteristic of weakness, so also is anger. For he who yields to pain and he who yields to anger, both are wounded and both submit.

But if you will, receive also a tenth present from the leader of the Muses [Apollo]: that to expect bad men not to do wrong is madness, for he who expects this desires an impossibility. But to allow men to behave so to others, and to expect them not to do you any wrong, is irrational and tyrannical.

19.   There are four principal aberrations of the superior faculty against which you should be constantly on your guard, and when you have detected them, you should wipe them out and say on each occasion: "This thought is not necessary; this tends to destroy social union; this which you are going to say comes not from the real thoughts", for you should consider it among the most absurd of things for a man not to speak from his real thoughts. But the fourth is when you shall reproach yourself for anything for this is an evidence of the diviner part within you being overpowered and yielding to the less honourable and to the perishable part, the body, and to its gross pleasures.

20.   Your aerial part and all the fiery parts which are min-gled in you, though by nature they have an upward tendency, still in obedience to the disposition of the universe they are overpowered here in the compound mass [the body]. And also the whole of the earthy part in you and the watery, though their tendency is downward, still are raised up and occupy a position which is not their natural one. In this manner then the elemen-tal parts obey the universal. For when they have been fixed in any place they necessarily remain there until again the univer-sal shall sound the signal for dissolution. Is it not then strange that your intelligent part only should be disobedient and dis-contented with its own place? And yet no force is imposed on it but only those things which are conformable to its nature. Still it does not submit but is carried in the opposite direction. For the movement towards injustice and intemperance and to

anger and grief and fear is nothing else than the act of one who deviates from nature. And also when the ruling faculty is discontented with anything that happens then too it deserts its post. For it is constituted for piety and reverence towards the gods no less than for justice. For these qualities also are comprehended under the generic term of contentment with the constitution of things and indeed they are prior to acts of justice.

21.   He who has not one and always the same object in life cannot be one and the same all through his life. But what I have said is not enough unless this also is added: what this object ought to be. For as there is not the same opinion about all the things which in some way or other are considered by the majority to be good but only about some certain things, that is, things which concern the common interest so also we ought to propose to ourselves an object which shall be of a common kind [social] and political. For he who directs all his own efforts to this object will make all his acts alike and thus will always be the same.

22.   Think of the country mouse and of the town mouse, and of the alarm and trepidation of the town mouse.

23.   Socrates used to call the opinions of the many by the name of Lamiae – bugbears to frighten children.

24.   The Lacedaemonians [Spartans] at their public spectacles used to set seats in the shade for strangers but themselves sat down anywhere.

25.   Socrates excused himself to Perdiccas for not going to him, saying, "It is because I would not perish by the worst of all ends"; that is, I would not receive a favour and then be unable to return it.

26. In the writings of the [Ephesians] there was this precept: constantly to think of some one of the men of former times who practised virtue.

27. The Pythagoreans bid us in the morning look to the heavens that we may be reminded of those bodies which continually do the same things and in the same manner perform their work, and also be reminded of their purity and nudity. For there is no veil over a star.

28. Consider what a man Socrates was when he dressed himself in a skin, after Xanthippe had taken his cloak and gone out, and what Socrates said to his friends who were ashamed of him and drew back from him when they saw him dressed thus.

29. Neither in writing nor in reading will you be able to lay down rules for others before you shall have first learned to obey rules yourself. Much more is this so in life.

30. A slave you are: free speech is not for you.

31. And my heart laughed within.
Odyssey, IX. 413.

32. And virtue they will curse, speaking harsh words.
HESIOD, *Works and Days*, 184.

33. To look for the fig in winter is the act of a madman and such is he who looks for his child when it is no longer allowed (Epictetus, iii. 24, 87).

34. When a man kisses his child, said Epictetus, he should whisper to himself, "Tomorrow perhaps you will die." – But those are words of bad omen. – "No word is a word of bad omen," said Epictetus, "which expresses any work of nature; or if it is so, it is also a word of bad omen to speak of the ears of corn being reaped" (Epictetus, iii. 24, 88).

35.   The unripe grape, the ripe bunch, the dried grape, are all changes, not into nothing, but into something which exists not yet (Epictetus, iii. 24).

36.   No man can rob us of our free will (Epictetus, iii. 22, 105).

37.   Epictetus also said, a man must discover an art [or rules] with respect to giving his assent. And in respect to his movements he must be careful that they are made with regard to circumstances, that they are consistent with social interests, and that they have regard to the value of the object. As to sensual desire, he should altogether keep away from it. And as to avoidance [aversion], he should not show it with respect to any of the things which are not in our power.

38.   "The dispute then," he said, "is not about any common matter but about being mad or not."

39.   Socrates used to say: What do you want, souls of rational men or irrational? – Souls of rational men. – Of what rational men, sound or unsound? – Sound. – Why then do you not seek for them? – Because we have them. – Why then do you fight and quarrel?

BOOK TWELVE

1. All those things at which you wish to arrive by a circuitous road you can have now, if you do not refuse them to yourself. And this means, if you will take no notice of all the past, and trust the future to providence, and direct the present only conformably to piety and justice. Conformably to piety that you may be content with the lot which is assigned to you, for nature designed it for you and you for it. Conformably to justice, that you may always speak the truth freely and without disguise, and do the things which are agreeable to law and according to the worth of each. And let neither another man's wickedness hinder you, nor opinion nor voice, nor yet the sensations of the poor flesh which has grown about you. For the passive part will look to this. If, then, whatever the time may be when you shall be near to your departure, neglecting everything else you shall respect only your ruling faculty and the divinity within you, and if you shall not be afraid because you must some time cease to live, but if you shall fear never to have begun to live according to nature then you will be a man worthy of the universe which has produced you and you will cease to be a stranger in your native land and to wonder at things which happen daily as if they were something unexpected, and to be dependent on this or that.

2. God sees the minds [ruling principles] of all men bared of the material vesture and skin and impurities. For

with his intellectual part alone he touches the intelligence only which has flowed and been derived from himself into these bodies. And if you also use yourself to do this, you will rid yourself of much trouble. For he who does not regard the poor flesh which envelops him, surely will not trouble himself by looking after fine clothing and dwelling and fame and other such externals and show.

3.   There are three things of which you are composed: a little body, a little breath [life], and intelligence. Of these the first two are yours so far as it is your duty to take care of them but the third alone is properly yours. Therefore if you shall separate from yourself, that is, from your understanding, whatever others do or say, and whatever you have done or said yourself, and whatever future things trouble you because they may happen, and whatever in the body which envelops you or in the breath [life], which is by nature associated with the body, is attached to you independent of your will, and whatever the external circumfluent vortex whirls round, so that the intellectual power exempt from the things of fate can live pure and free by itself, doing what is just and accepting what happens and saying the truth. If you will separate, I say, from this ruling faculty the things which are attached to it by the impressions of sense, and the things of time to come and of time that is past, and will make yourself like Empedocles' sphere,

All round, and in its joyous rest reposing; and if you shall strive to live only what is really your life – that is, the present – then you will be able to pass that portion of life which remains for you up to the time of your death free from perturbations, nobly, and obedient to your own daemon [to the god that is within you].

4. I have often wondered how it is that every man loves himself more than all the rest of men, but yet sets less value on his own opinion of himself than on the opinion of others. If then a god or a wise teacher should present himself to a man and bid him to think of nothing and to design nothing which he would not express as soon as he conceived it, he could not endure it even for a single day. So much more respect do we have to what our neighbours think of us than to what we think of ourselves.

5. How can it be that the gods, after having arranged all things well and benevolently for mankind, have overlooked this alone, that some men, and very good men, and men who, as we may say, have had most communion with the divinity, and through pious acts and religious observances have been most intimate with the divinity, when they have once died should never exist again, but should be completely extinguished?

But if this is so, be assured that if it ought to have been otherwise, the gods would have done it. For if it were just, it would also be possible and if it were according to nature, nature would have had it so. But because it is not so, if in fact it is not so, be convinced that it ought not to have been so. For you see even of yourself that in this inquiry you are disputing with the Deity. And we should not be able to dispute with the gods like this unless they were most excellent and most just but if this is so they would not have allowed anything in the ordering of the universe to be neglected unjustly and irrationally.

6. Practise yourself even in the things which you despair of accomplishing. For even the left hand, which is ineffectual for all other things for want of practice, holds the bridle more vigorously than the right hand for it has been practised in this.

7.   Consider in what condition both in body and soul a man should be when he is overtaken by death. And consider the shortness of life, the boundless abyss of time past and future, the feebleness of all matter.

8.   Contemplate the formative principles [forms] of things bare of their coverings, the purposes of actions, consider what pain is, what pleasure is, and death, and fame, who is to himself the cause of his uneasiness, how no man is hindered by another, that everything is opinion.

9.   In the application of your principles you must be like the pancratiast, not like the gladiator. For the gladiator lets fall the sword which he uses and is killed but the other always has his hand, and needs to do nothing else than use it.

10.   See what things are in themselves, dividing them into matter, form, and purpose.

11.   What a power man has to do nothing except what God will approve, and to accept all that God may give him.

12.   With respect to that which happens conformably to nature, we ought to blame neither gods, for they do nothing wrong either voluntarily or involuntarily, nor men, for they do nothing wrong except involuntarily. Consequently we should blame nobody.

13.   How ridiculous and what a stranger he is who is surprised at anything which happens in life.

14.   Either there is a fatal necessity and invincible order, or a kind providence, or a confusion without a purpose and without a director (iv. 27). If then there is an invincible necessity, why do you resist? But if there is a providence which allows itself to be appeased, make yourself worthy of the help of the divinity. But if there is a confusion without a governor, be

content that in such a tempest you have in yourself a certain ruling intelligence. And even if the tempest carries you away, let it carry away the poor flesh, the poor breath, everything else – for the intelligence at least it will not carry away.

15.   Does the light of the lamp shine without losing its splendour until it is extinguished? And shall the truth which is in you and justice and temperance be extinguished [before your death]?

16.   When a man has presented the appearance of having done wrong [say], "How then do I know if this is a wrongful act? And even if he has done wrong, how do I know that he has not condemned himself?" And so this is like tearing his own face. Consider that he who would not have the bad man do wrong, is like the man who would not have the fig tree to bear juice in the figs, and infants to cry, and the horse to neigh, and whatever else must necessarily be. For what must a man do who has such a character? If then you are irritable, cure this man's disposition.

17.   If it is not right, do not do it: if it is not true, do not say it. [For let your efforts be—]

18.   In everything always observe what the thing is which produces for you an appearance, and resolve it by dividing it into the formal, the material, the purpose, and the time within which it must end.

19.   Perceive at last that you have in you something better and more divine than the things which cause the various affects, and as it were pull you by the strings. What is there now in my mind – is it fear, or suspicion, or desire, or anything of the kind?

20. First, do nothing inconsiderately, nor without a purpose. Second, make your acts refer to nothing else than to a social end.

21. Consider that before long you will be nobody and nowhere, nor will any of the things exist which you now see, nor any of those who are now living. For all things are formed by nature to change and be turned and to perish, in order that other things in continuous succession may exist.

22. Consider that everything is opinion, and opinion is in your power. Take away then, when you choose, your opinion, and like a mariner who has rounded the promontory, you will find calm, everything stable, and a waveless bay.

23. Any one activity, whatever it may be, when it has ceased at its proper time, suffers no evil because it has ceased. Neither does someone who has done this act suffer any evil for this reason, that the act has ceased. In like manner then the whole, which consists of all the acts, which is our life, if it ceases at its proper time, suffers no evil for this reason, that it has ceased. Neither has he who terminates this series at the proper time been dealt with badly. But the proper time and the limit nature fixes, sometimes as in old age the peculiar nature of man, but always the universal nature, by the change of whose parts the whole universe continues ever young and perfect. And everything which is useful to the universal is always good and in season. Therefore the termination of life for every man is no evil, because neither is it shameful, since it is both independent of the will and not opposed to the general interest, but it is good, since it is seasonable, and profitable to and congruent with the universal. For thus too he is moved by the Deity

who is moved in the same manner with the Deity, and moved towards the same thing in his mind.

24. These three principles you must keep ready: In your actions, do nothing either inconsiderately or otherwise than as justice herself would act; with respect to what may happen to you from without, consider that it happens either by chance or according to providence, and you must neither blame chance nor accuse providence. Second, consider what every being is from the seed to the time of its receiving a soul, and from the reception of a soul to the giving back of the same, and of what things every being is compounded, and into what things it is resolved. Third, if you should suddenly be raised up above the earth, and look down on human things, and observe how great is the variety of them, and at the same time also should see at a glance how great is the number of beings who dwell all around in the air and the ether, consider that as often as you should be raised up, you would see the same things, sameness of form and shortness of duration. Are these things of which to be proud?

25. Cast away opinion: you are saved. Who then hinders you from casting it away?

26. When you are troubled about anything, you have forgotten this, that all things happen according to the universal nature. And forgotten that a man's wrongful act is nothing to you. And further you have forgotten that everything which happens always happened so and will happen so again, and now happens so everywhere. You have forgotten also how close the kinship is between a man and the whole human race, for it is a community not of mere blood or seed but of intelligence. And you have forgotten too that every man's intelligence is a

god and is an outflowing of the Deity. And forgotten that nothing is a man's own but that his child and his body and his very soul came from the Deity. You have forgotten that everything is opinion. And lastly you have forgotten that every man lives the present time only and loses only this.

27.   Constantly bring to your recollection those who have complained greatly about anything, those who have been most conspicuous by the greatest fame or misfortunes or enmities or fortunes of any kind. Then ask yourself where they all are now. Smoke and ash and a tale, or not even a tale. And let there be present to your mind also everything of this sort: how Fabius Catellinus lived in the country, and Lucius Lupus in his gardens, and Stertinius at Briae, and Tiberius at Capreae, and Velius Rufus [or Rufus at Velia]. Indeed, think of the eager pursuit of anything conjoined with pride and how worthless everything is after which men violently strain and how much more philosophical it is for a man, when the opportunity arises, to show himself just, temperate, obedient to the gods. And to do this with all simplicity: for the pride which is proud of its want of pride is the most intolerable of all.

28.   To those who ask, "Where have you seen the gods, or how do you comprehend that they exist and so worship them", I answer, in the first place, they may be seen even with the eyes; in the second place, neither have I seen even my own soul, and yet I honour it. Thus with respect to the gods, from what I constantly experience of their power, I comprehend that they exist, and I worship them.

29.   The safety of life is this, to examine everything all through, what it is itself, that is its material, what the formal part is; with all your soul to do justice and to say the truth.

What remains, except to enjoy life by joining one good thing to another so as not to leave even the smallest intervals between?

30. There is one light of the sun, though it is interrupted by walls, mountains, and infinite other things. There is one common substance, though it is distributed among countless bodies which have their individual qualities. There is one soul, though it is distributed among infinite natures and individual circumscriptions [or individuals]. There is one intelligent soul, though it seems to be divided. Now in the things which have been mentioned, all the other parts, such as those which are air and matter, are without sensation and have no bond and yet even these parts the intelligent principle holds together and the gravitation towards the same. But intellect in a peculiar manner tends to that which is of the same kin, and combines with it, and the feeling for communion is not interrupted.

31. What do you wish – to continue to exist? Well, do you wish to have sensation, movement, growth, and then again to cease to grow, to use your speech, to think? What is there of all these things which seems to you worth desiring? But if it is easy to set little value on all these things, turn to that which remains, which is to follow reason and God. But it is inconsistent with honouring reason and God to be troubled because by death a man will be deprived of the other things.

32. How small a part of the boundless and unfathomable time is assigned to every man, for it is very soon swallowed up in the eternal! And how small a part of the whole substance, and how small a part of the universal soul, and on what a small clod of the whole earth you creep! Reflecting on all this, consider nothing to be great, except to act as your nature leads you, and to endure that which the common nature brings.

33.   How does the ruling faculty make use of itself for all lies in this? But everything else, whether it is in the power of your will or not, is only lifeless ashes and smoke.

34.   This reflection is most adapted to move us to contempt of death, that even those who think pleasure to be a good and pain an evil have still despised it.

35.   The man to whom only that which comes in due season is good, and to whom it is the same thing whether he has done more or fewer acts conformable to right reason, and to whom it makes no difference whether he contemplates the world for a longer or a shorter time – for this man, death is not a terrible thing either (iii. 7; vi. 23; x. 20; xii. 23).

36.   Man, you have been a citizen in this great state [the world]. What difference does it make to you whether for five years [or three]? For that which is conformable to the laws is just for all. Where is the hardship then, if no tyrant nor yet an unjust judge sends you away from the state, but nature, who brought you into it? The same as if a praetor who has employed an actor dismisses him from the stage. "But I have not finished the five acts, but only three of them." You speak well, but in life the three acts are the whole drama for what shall be a complete drama is determined by him who was once the cause of its composition, and now of its dissolution but you are the cause of neither. Depart satisfied therefore, for he is also satisfied who releases you.